Alan Palmer, a retired schoolmaster, was for sixteen years head of the history department at Highgate School, London. He has written more than twenty-five books. Among them are the *Penguin Dictionary of Modern History*, the *Penguin Dictionary of Twentieth Century History 1900–1989*, four books concerned with the modern history of south-eastern Europe, and lives of Metternich, George IV, Tsar Alexander I, Frederick the Great, Bismarck and Kaiser Wilhelm II. His most recent biography is *Bernadotte; Napoleon's Marshal, Sweden's King*. At present he is working on a history of the later years of the Ottoman Empire.

John Campbell is a freelance historian and political biographer. His books include *Lloyd George: The Goat in the Wilderness* (1977); *F.E. Smith, First Earl of Birkenhead* (1983); *Roy Jenkins* (1983); *Nye Bevan and the Mirage of British Socialism* (1987). He is currently writing a biography of Edward Heath. He also edited *The Experience of World War II* (1989). He is married with two children and lives in London.

Other titles in the series *Makers of the Twentieth Century* in Cardinal:

Brandt   Barbara Marshall
de Gaulle   Julian Jackson
Deng Xiaoping   David Goodman
Martin Luther King   Adam Fairclough
Nkrumah   David Birmingham
Roosevelt   Fiona Venn
Khrushchev   Martin McCauley

Forthcoming titles in the same series:

Trotsky   David Law
Tito   Stevan K. Pavlowitch
Nehru   Denis Judd
Jinnah   Howard Brasted
Smuts   Iain Smith
Lenin   Beryl Williams
Adenauer   Andrew Crozier

Makers of the Twentieth Century

Kemal
Atatürk

ALAN PALMER

SERIES EDITOR
JOHN CAMPBELL

CARDÍNAL

A CARDINAL Book

First published in Great Britain in Cardinal by Sphere Books Ltd 1991

Typeset by Leaper & Gard Ltd, Bristol
Printed and bound in Great Britain by
Cox & Wyman Ltd, Reading

ISBN 0 7474 0563 8

Sphere Books Ltd
A Division of
Macdonald & Co (Publishers) Ltd
Orbit House
1 New Fetter Lane
London EC4A 1AR
A member of Maxwell Macmillan Pergamon Publishing Corporation

Contents

Editor's Foreword

The last decade of the century is a good moment to look back at some of the dominating individuals who have shaped the modern world. *Makers of the Twentieth Century* is a series of short biographical reassessments, written by specialists but aimed at a wide general audience. We hope that they will be useful to sixth-formers and students seeking a brief introduction to a new subject; but also to the ordinary reader looking for the minimum she or he needs to know of the life and legacy of the century's key figures, in a form that can be absorbed in a single sitting. At the same time we hope that the interpretations, based on the latest research – even where there is not space to display it – will be of sufficient interest to command the attention of other specialists.

The series will eventually cover all the outstanding heroes and villains of the century. They can, as a kind of party game, be sorted into three – or perhaps four – types. Some can be classed primarily as national leaders, who either restored the failing destinies of old nations (de Gaulle, Adenauer, Kemal Atatürk) or created new ones out of the collapse of the European empires (Nkrumah, Jinnah). Others were national leaders first of all, but made a still greater impact on the international stage (Franklin Roosevelt, Willy Brandt, Jan Smuts). A further category were not heads of government at all, but achieved worldwide resonance as the embodiments of powerful ideas (Trotsky, Martin Luther King). The great tyrants, however, (Hitler, Stalin, Mao Zedong) are not easily contained in any category but transcend them all.

The series, too, aims to leap categories, attempting to place each subject in a double focus, both in relation to the domestic politics of his or her own country and as an actor on the world stage – whether as builder or destroyer, role model or prophet. One consequence of the communications revolution in this century has been that the charismatic leaders of quite small countries (Castro, Ho Chi Minh, Gadaffi) can command a following well beyond the frontiers of their national constituency.

At the centre of each volume stands the individual: of course biography can be a distorting mirror, exaggerating the influence of human agency on vast impersonal events; yet unquestionably there are, as Shakespeare's Brutus observed, tides in the affairs of men 'which, taken at the flood, lead on to fortune'. At critical moments the course of history can be diverted, channelled or simply ridden by individuals who by luck, ruthlessness or destiny are able to impose their personality, for good or ill, upon their times. Who can doubt that Lenin and Hitler, Mao and Gorbachev – to name but four – have decisively, at least for a time, bent the history of our epoch to their will? These, with men and women from every major country in the world, are the *Makers of the Twentieth Century.*

John Campbell
London, 1990

Chronology

1881   Born as Mustafa, son of Ali Riza, at Salonika

c. 1894   Receives additional name Kemal at school in Salonika

1895–99   Cadet at Monastir (Bitolj)

March 1899   Becomes officer cadet at Harbiye War College, Constantinople

January 1905   Passes out of War College as a Staff Captain

1905–7   Serving in Syria

September 1907   Posted to Salonika garrison

July 1908   With Enver in Salonika when Young Turks force constitution from Sultan Abdul Hamid

April 1909   Supports deposition of Abdul Hamid

October 1911   A Major in Libya, in war against Italy

1912–13   Balkan Wars; helps recapture Adrianople from Bulgarians

October 1913   Military attaché in Sofia (Bulgaria)

February 1915   Commands XIXth Division in Gallipoli peninsula

25 April 1915   Opposes allied landings at Ari Burnu

1916   Commands Sixteenth Army at Diyarbakir, with rank of General and Pasha

July–October 1917   Commands Seventh Army in Syria but clashes with General von Falkenhayn

15 December 1917   Accompanies Turkish heir to the throne on a mission to Germany (until 5 January 1918)

August 1918   Returns to Seventh Army command

19 May 1919   Begins Nationalist Revolution at Samsun

September 1919   Presides over Nationalist Congress at Sivas which confirms the National Pact

23 April 1920   Opening session of the first Grand National Assembly, Ankara

August–September 1921   Greek advance into Anatolia checked at battle of the Sakarya River

9 September 1922   Turkish recapture of Smyrna (Izmir) marks defeat of Greek invasion of Anatolia

September–October 1922   Chanak Crisis

1 November 1922   Kemal proclaims the abolition of the Sultanate

24 July 1923   Treaty of Lausanne establishes the new Turkey's frontiers

9 October 1923   Ankara becomes Turkish capital

29 October 1923   Proclamation of Turkish Republic, with Kemal as first President

3 March 1924   Abolition of Caliphate

17 February 1926   New Civil Code

July 1926   Alleged assassination plot at Izmir leads to purge of Opposition and to public executions

15–20 October 1927   Kemal's 'Great Speech', Ankara

November 1928   Introduction of the Latin Alphabet

29 November 1934   Law requiring surnames leads Kemal to become 'Atatürk'

10 November 1938   Dies at Dolmabahçe Palace, Istanbul

10 November 1953   Atatürk's remains interred in the Anitkabir, Ankara

Abbreviations

CUP Committee of Union and Progress
RPP Republican People's Party

Alternative Place-Names

(Old versions precede contemporary names)

In modern Turkey
Adalkia: Antalya
Adrianople: Edirne
Alexandretta: Iskenderun
Angora: Ankara
Antioch: Antakya
Brusa: Bursa
Caesarea: Kayseri
Chanak: Çanakkale
Constantinople: Istanbul
Euphrates: Firat
Gallipoli: Gelibolu
Mudania: Mudanya
Pera/Galata: Beyoğlu
Smyrna: Izmir
Scutari: Üsküdar
Tigris: Dicle
Trebizond: Trabzond

In Greece
Salonika: Thessaloniki

In Syria
Aleppo: Halab
Damascus: Esh Sham

In Yugoslavia
Monastir: Bitolj
Üsküb: Skopje

The Turkish Republic 1938

BLACK

BULGARIA

Eastern
Thrace

GREECE Edirne   Chatalja

Zonguldak

Bosphorus

İstanbul   Izmit

Sea of Marmara   Yalova

Gallipoli   Mudania   *R. Sakarya*

Canakkale   Bursa   Ankara

Inonu   Eskishehir

Chesme.

Izmir   Afyon
Karahisar

R. Menderes   Konya

Antalya   Mers

DODECANESE

RHODES

CYPRUS

0   50   100   150   200 miles   --- Main railways

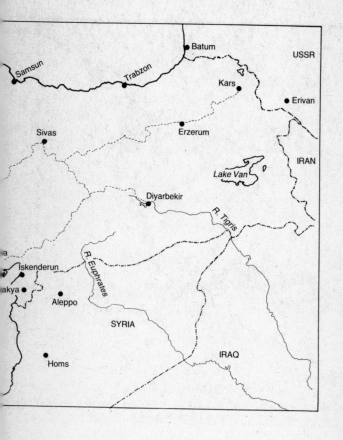

Istanbul

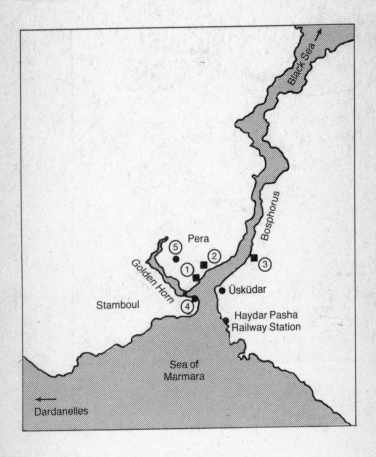

KEY

① DOLMABAHÇE PALACE   ④ SARAYBURNU

② YILDIZ PALACE   ⑤ HARBIYE

③ BEYLERBEY PALACE

The Gallipoli Campaign 1915

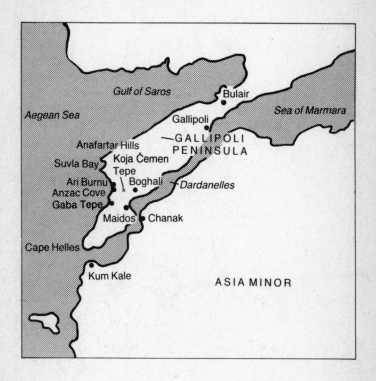

Introduction

Some men and women from the past stand out in the mind because, for good or evil, their names are branded on an era of history. To mention them is to conjure up images which we feel we have known for a long time: Augustus, Charlemagne, Elizabeth I, Cromwell, Napoleon, for example; or in the twentieth century Lenin, Hitler, Roosevelt, de Gaulle and Mao Zedong. In such company the octosyllabic Mustafa Kemal Atatürk sounds unfamiliar. He did not export a revolution, embark on wars of conquest, or shine at the centre of a cultural galaxy. Yet anyone visiting Turkey today, more than half a century after his death, can see from a plethora of monuments and street-names how deeply his personality is impressed upon the republic of which he was such an awesome founding father. Kemal Atatürk ranks high among the Makers of the Twentieth Century on four counts: as a soldier whose skills on the battlefield twice decided the pattern of world history; as the most ruthless modernizer of an archaic society since Peter the Great; as a statesman who guided the political institutions he created through their formative years; and as the proto-type authoritarian ruler for a post-imperial and secularist

1

Asia and Africa. It is tempting to say of Atatürk, as Goethe once said of Napoleon, that 'His life was the stride of a demigod'.

In 1881, the year of Kemal Atatürk's birth, the Turkish Empire was ruled by Sultan Abdul Hamid II, the thirty-fourth sovereign of the House of Osman. The dynasty had its origins in a tribe of converts to Islam who, in the fourteenth and early fifteenth centuries, fought their way to the top in Anatolia, crossed the Dardanelles into south-eastern Europe and, in 1453, captured Constantinople and replaced the crumbling Eastern Orthodox Byzantine Empire with a new Islamic superpower. The Sultans soon became masters of Asia Minor, of North Africa from the Nile delta to Algiers and Oran, and of the Danube Basin and the Balkans. With the decline of Tartar power they added to their lands the Crimea and the steppes between the Dniester and the Volga. They assumed, too, a spiritual authority of great significance in 1517 when Sultan Selim I, having seized Egypt from the Mamelukes, received a deputation from the Arab ruler of Mecca who offered him the keys of Islam's Holy City and the long-lapsed title of Caliph, Protector of the Faithful. It was not until the eighteenth century that the Sultans made full use of this title, claiming a universal headship over Islam which was disputed by sects in Persia and the Indian sub-continent.

Whether or not the Sultans called themselves Caliph, by Shakespeare's day 'the Turk' had become the embodiment of militant Islam. The Sultan's soldiery constituted a standing menace to the rulers of Christendom, while his seamen remained the scourge of the Mediterranean. As late as 1683 a force of 200,000 Turks besieged Vienna for sixty days, penetrating even further into lower Austria until they threatened the borders of Bavaria. Thereafter Islam went on the defensive in eastern Europe. Wars ravaged the region frequently in the hundred years which followed the siege of Vienna. Yet much of the fighting was indecisive. On three occasions the Austrians captured Belgrade, only to lose the city each time to the Turks. Moreover, although Russia first reached the Black Sea in 1696 when Peter the Great captured Azov, it was another eighty years before the armies of Catherine the Great consolidated these gains and, by the Treaty of Kuchuk Kainardji of 1774, secured for the sovereigns of the Russian Empire a protective right over the Orthodox Christians living in Constantinople. Most European statesmen assumed that, since the Ottoman Empire had been created solely by military conquest, defeat on land and sea would speedily lead to its disintegration.

But was this desirable? What would succeed the Ottoman Empire? Neither the British nor the French wished to see Russia become a Mediterranean Power; 'Constantinople is the centre of world empire,' Napoleon remarked confidentially to his secretary in 1807, during his Tilsit summit conference with Tsar Alexander I. Some Russians, too, were apprehensive, even though there were twelve wars between Russia and Turkey in the course of a century. In 1829 Count Nesselrode, the shrewdest foreign minister of the Tsars, succeeded in convincing Nicholas I that it would be wiser to prop up Turkey, for to seek a solution of the Eastern Question would 'plunge one into a labyrinth of difficulty and complications each one more inextricable than the other'.[1] Briefly, for some twenty or thirty years, the Sultans had the opportunity to modernize their system of government and satisfy the European Great Powers of the value of an international guarantee upholding the independence and integrity of the Ottoman lands; and by the 'Gulhane Decree' of November 1839 Sultan Abdul Mejid I inaugurated an era of legislative reforms known as the *Tanzimat-i-Hayriye* – which might be translated as 'Auspicious Restructuring', for *Tanzimat* is almost identical in meaning with the Russian *Perestroika*.

By 1839 Great Britain and France already enjoyed the

advantages of a well-developed form of parliamentary government; the other three major powers (Austria, Russia and Prussia) had become centralized autocracies, possessing effective councils of ministers who advised the sovereign on policy at home and abroad. The *Tanzimat* did not give the Ottoman Empire a constitution, but it did at least introduce comprehensive codes of law, departments of state and a consultative privy council which could support or oppose the executive initiatives of the Grand Vizier, the traditional title of the Sultan's first minister. Unfortunately the authority of successive Sultans in Constantinople itself remained weak, while their administrative officials in distant dependencies continued to wield a power which was becoming increasingly independent. As the Serbian and Greek struggles for national recognition had already shown, too often local pashas abused that power with acts of capricious cruelty.

The Sultan's failure to make the *Tanzimat* a basis for effective government convinced Turkey's most powerful neighbour that the Ottoman Empire was decrepit and unlikely to hold together much longer. Tsar Nicholas I reversed his policy, wrongly counting on what he believed to be a sympathetic government in London. In January 1853, as a conversational aside to a British diplomat when he was leaving a private concert in St Petersburg, Nicholas I coined the over-quoted metaphor of 'a sick man on our hands' to describe the condition of the Ottoman Empire.[2] But instead of agreement on a contingency plan for the invalid's demise – as Nicholas had hoped – the Russian, Turkish, British and French governments blundered into a senseless conflict. The Crimean War, and the Peace Treaty of Paris in 1856, bolstered up the sick man rather than buried him. The Sultan gave yet another undertaking of reform in return for promises of foreign capital. Financially Turkey became dependent on the West, with new banking institutions linked closely to Paris and London; the Ottoman Bank, founded in

Constantinople in 1863, had a Frenchman as its director and an Englishman as his deputy. It is therefore not surprising that when, at the start of the Great Eastern Crisis of 1875–78, a new wave of repression by Turkish irregular troops in the Balkans provoked protests from humanitarians in the West as well as in Russia, the British and French governments backed the Ottoman authorities. For yet a third time a sultan committed himself to reform: at the height of the crisis the enlightened grand vizier, Midhat Pasha, secured from Abdul Hamid II a written constitution, not only providing basic civic rights but promising a bicameral parliament, with a nominated senate and a chamber of deputies elected by men over the age of twenty-four.

The first Ottoman parliament was formally opened by the Sultan on 19 March 1877. Ominously Abdul Hamid II had dismissed Midhat a month before, fearing that his western ways would seek to convert the sultanate into a constitutional monarchy. Parliament became a talking shop. After eleven months it was dissolved, with little accomplished. Not until thirty years later – in December 1908 – did pressure from the Young Turk reformers induce the ageing and incorrigible Abdul Hamid to recall Parliament and, in his own words, 'proclaim the Constitution anew'. By then a sense of Turkish nationhood, hardly articulate in 1878, was beginning to make an impact in political life. No one had as yet perceived that, if analyzed logically, Turkish nationalism was incompatible with allegiance to a supranational Ottoman Empire or with acceptance of a strict, all-embracing concept of Islam. Not least among the achievements of Kemal Atatürk was to find a resolution of these impossible loyalties.

'That Turkey is weak, fanatical, and misgoverned no one can honestly deny,' declared Stratford de Redcliffe in a book published in 1881, the year of Atatürk's birth.[3] The most famous and Turkophile of British ambassadors penned this final damning verdict on an empire he had known for seventy years not long before his death. He argued that the Sultan's restless extravagance was bringing Turkey to financial ruin, that the promised reforms remained mere paper pledges, and that the great powers had a right – perhaps even a duty – to occupy Constantinople and impose reforms and honest government. Had Stratford's drastic policy been pursued, the lives of thousands of the Sultan's Christian subjects might have been spared; in particular, there would have been no massacre of Armenians in Constantinople in 1896, an event as repugnant to liberals in the West as the tragedy of Tiananmen Square nearly a century later. Foreign soldiers and marines did indeed move into Constantinople, Macedonia and Crete for several months at a time during the years in which Kemal was growing into manhood. Their coming helped restore order in an empire whose government could not adequately police even the capital itself. But their presence – like the Sultan's subsequent resort to German and British 'advisers' at the head of his army and his navy – intensified the xenophobic sense of frustration already influencing the more intelligent members of the younger generation.

Despite Stratford de Redcliffe's criticism of Turkish rule, the empire into which Kemal was born still looked impressive on the map, straddling the meeting point of three continents. In 1881 the crescent flag of the Ottomans flew over northern Greece, Crete, Albania and much of present-day Yugoslavia as well as over Medina, Jerusalem, Damascus and Baghdad, in the Lebanon and Libya, and as far south as the headwaters of the Persian Gulf and the Red Sea coast of Arabia. But, in an age of imperfect communication, the sheer extent of the Ottoman Empire was a source of weakness rather than of strength. A coastal voyage from the Bosphorus to Beirut could take a month, and so, too, could the crossing to

Tripoli or Benghazi although there were steamers able to make the journey within a week. The railway network was incomplete. Lines linking the Sultan's capital with his eastern frontiers, with Palestine and with Baghdad were still not completed when his empire fell apart. Kemal Atatürk was to bring cohesion and sound government to a republican Turkey by accepting the loss of all these outlying territories. And from a war of independence fought to secure the inner heartland of Anatolia he was able to cherish the growth of a new national pride.

Soldier of the Sultan

1

Mustafa Kemal Atatürk was born, not in the Turkish lands where his name is remembered, but in the second largest city of modern Greece, the port of Salonika. This is not so surprising as it seems. For, despite the city's Hellenistic origins and Byzantine heritage, Salonika was the administrative centre of a Turkish province and, being little more than 300 miles from Constantinople, it was close enough to respond readily to any change in the political mood of the capital. Salonika, and the cluster of villages round it, still looked overwhelmingly Turkish in character. A traveller sailing up the Gulf of Salonika could see at its head the seven towers of the Sultan's fortress on Mount Khortiatis and, beneath them, more than twenty tapering minarets beside the domes of churches which were converted into mosques 400 years before.[1] It was in a small pink house close to the oldest of these former churches that Zubeyde, the wife of Ali Riza, gave birth to a boy on an unknown winter's day early in 1881, the fifth year of Abdul Hamid II's reign. Ali Riza insisted that his son should be called Mustafa, after a brother of his who died in infancy.

When the Turks were at war with Russia in 1877 Ali

8

Riza served as a militia officer, but by 1881 he was a customs clerk, like Hitler's father eight years later in Austria. The post gave him a certain social standing, and his house on the hill above the Arch of Galerius looked solidly comfortable, more impressive than most dwellings in this Ahmet Subasi district. He was forty-two, shrewd and even-tempered, mildly cynical over religious observance, respected as a literate person who supplemented a regular salary with profits from a small timber business. When Mustafa was born, Zubeyde was still well under thirty, the hot-tempered daughter of an Albanian peasant farmer whose family came from south-eastern Anatolia. These Anatolian origins explain Zubeyde's blue eyes and fair hair, features which Mustafa was to inherit. Zubeyde could neither read nor write, but she was ambitious for her son, especially as she had already lost four children, who had been either stillborn or unable to fight the diseases of infancy; a surviving daughter, Makbule, counted for little in her mother's reckoning, as was so often the case in Turkish families under the sultanate. Ali Riza wished Mustafa to be a merchant; Zubeyde believed he would make a good priest, and he began his education under a hoja (a religious teacher of the Koran) at a school attached to a mosque. But Salonika possessed a model state school newly opened and run by a gifted teacher, Semsi Effendi; and within a few days his shrewd father had secured a place for Mustafa there. The difference between lessons at the mosque and lessons at Semsi Effendi's school was so striking that the contrast moulded the lasting convictions of the youngster more effectively than any formal instruction. By the age of seven Mustafa was well on the way to becoming a natural secularist.

'Soon afterwards, my father died,' Mustafa recalled in 1922.[2] Ali Riza had begun to drink heavily and his health gave way completely. When he died a few months later there was no money to be handed on to Zubeyde. She was forced to sell the house on the hill in Salonika and take Makbule and Mustafa to her brother's farm near Langaza, eighteen miles east of the city. There the townboy sensed, for the first time, the uncertainties of peasant agriculture in a bleak and barren countryside; it was yet another experience which left a mark on his thinking thirty years later.

A neighbour's son, Ahmet, had been accepted as a cadet at the military school in Salonika. Mustafa, who despised Ahmet, wished to go there himself, having no doubt that he could surpass Ahmet and, for that matter, other young aspirants to social advancement in Turkish Macedonia, too. With the backing of his uncle and an army officer who had been a friend of Ali Riza, Mustafa followed Ahmet to the military school. He progressed brilliantly in his studies. So good was he at mathematics that one instructor, who took the fatherless lad under his wing, began to call him 'Kemal' ('Perfection'). The name stuck and it was as 'Mustafa Kemal' that the boy from the Ahmet Subasi district climbed the ladder of promotion.

At fourteen he was both a dandy and a prig, hostile to his mother for marrying again – on this occasion to a minor official in the tobacco trade. So affronted was Kemal that for him the officer corps became a substitute family. In 1895 he went on eagerly from Salonika to the more advanced military school in the carpet-making town of Monastir (later renamed Bitolj) in Yugoslavia. His excellence at mathematics was maintained. He began to read widely, too: the patriotic romanticism of the Turkish poet, Namik Kemal, appealed to him strongly; and he went beyond the prescribed historical works of the military colleges, becoming fascinated by Napoleon's campaigns in Egypt and Syria, although he was highly critical of Napoleon himself.

He did not, however, read only Turkish authors. At Monastir he became a close friend of Ali Fethi, a slim and elegant cadet slightly older than himself, from neighbouring Ochrid. Fethi, who possessed a certain cosmopolitan charm and self-assurance, already spoke French well. It was, he maintained, the proper tongue for those who aspired to intellectual emancipation, and Kemal dutifully sought special coaching in French from a Dominican monk. Before long he was writing French verse. Either at Monastir, or soon afterwards, he began to study German too. Like so many of their contemporaries in central Europe, Russia, and the Mediterranean lands, Mustafa Kemal and Ali Fethi became intellectual revolutionaries. Yet, although the young Kemal conscientiously made some notes on socialism, the prophets who appealed most to the two cadets were not Marx, Bakunin or Kropotkin but the political philisophers of eighteenth-century France. At Monastir in the late 1890s Kemal was reading books which in the early 1780s had fired the mind of the young Bonaparte at his military academy in Brienne. In later years Kemal was influenced by the mid-century positivism of Auguste Comte, but it is hardly surprising if 'Kemalism' – a pragmatic creed which he never systematically formulated – owes more to Rousseau and the fulfilment of the general will than to any other source of inspiration.

Had Kemal's education taken him straight from Salonika to Constantinople, it is probable that such dissentient beliefs would never have become implanted in his mind at so formative an age. Monastir, however, was a remote military college on the Empire's north-western frontier, far from the centre of Ottoman government: while military discipline was strict, the broader extra-mural studies benefited from tolerant supervision and incompetence; it was assumed that it was admirable for cadets to read French or German, irrespective of the subject matter which they studied. Mustafa Kemal passed his final examinations at Monastir with high grades. Inevitably he was marked out for further specialist training. He joined the 1899 infantry class at Harbiye, the war college in the Pera (now known as Beyoğlu) district of Constantinople, Ottoman Turkey's equivalent of Britain's Sandhurst or America's West Point. 'A brilliant although difficult young man, with whom it is impossible to achieve any intimacy,' was the commandant's final assessment of Kemal at Monastir.[3]

Kemal arrived at Harbiye in the second week of March 1899, newly commissioned as a junior lieutenant. It was his first visit to Constantinople, for so many centuries the capital of great empires. The Harbiye Barracks were about a mile north of Sultan Abdul Hamid II's official residence, the Dolmabahçe Palace beside the Bosphorus, and a mile and a half west of the Yildiz Kiosk which, by 1899, had become the Sultan's favourite home. Around the barracks in Pera and a succession of small villages up the Bosphorus the wealthier cadets and instructors could enjoy a rich social life. Not, however, Kemal; with one exception, the gates of the pashas' waterfront villas remained closed to the intruder from Salonika. Only Ali Fuad, a general's son who had spent most of his life in Constantinople, became as close a friend as Fethi had been at Monastir. Occasionally Kemal visited Fuad's family home at Kuzguncuk, on the Asian shore, looking across the waters to the Corinthian grandeur of the Dolmabahçe Palace. But, for the most part, he was a lone figure. On some nights he drank too much raki and satisfied his natural lust in sleazy alleys across the Galata Bridge. Yet week after week he concentrated on his military studies, taking particular care to improve his French and German. Once again there were no complaints from his instructors about his diligence; and in 1902 he was picked for specialist training as a staff officer. A great future in service to 'the Shadow of God on Earth' seemed to await him. As yet, however, the Sultan remained for Kemal a symbolic figure whom he might see occasionally at Yildiz in a postilioned carriage escorted by Lancers on his way from palace to mosque for Friday prayers.

Kemal was a shrewd observer of life around him. When he arrived in Constantinople in 1899 German infiltration of Turkish business and trade was at its peak. In that spring the Sultan formally authorized German investors and engineers to construct a railway linking the Bosphorus to the Persian Gulf, the famous Berlin–Baghdad project. Already a German company was building harbour works at Scutari (now known as Üsküdar) on the Asiatic shore, facing Constantinople itself, and 250 miles of German-laid track ran across Anatolia from Eskişehir to Konya, a region Kemal came to know well in later years. For most of the nineteenth century British influence had prevailed in Constantinople, yet no reigning British sovereign had ever paid a courtesy call on a sultan. By contrast the ruler of Imperial Germany, Kaiser Wilhelm II, had twice been Abdul Hamid's guest: a short visit in 1889 was followed by an ostentatious journey to Constantinople, Jerusalem and Damascus in October and November 1898.

The Kaiser's 'expedition to the Orient' created a sensation.[4] Other monarchs had ostracized Sultan Abdul Hamid for his failure to save his Armenian Christian subjects from massacre over the past three years. Wilhelm II, however, was fascinated by Islam: three hundred million Moslems could 'rest assured that the German Kaiser will ever be their friend', he declared when he visited the tomb of Saladin in Damascus. There had been German military instructors on the Bosphorus and in Anatolia since the Kaiser's first visit; now their number and influence were increased. Inevitably the orders for weapons needed to modernize the Sultan's military machine went to Krupps and other German firms. Traditionally the Turkish navy had looked to Britain for warships and training, but in 1899 there was not a single seaworthy vessel in the Bosphorus. If, after years of total neglect, the Sultan sought to create a new fleet, he might turn again to Britain – or strengthen still more his contacts with Germany.

Kemal was prepared to learn from Germany. He translated into Turkish a German manual on infantry training; originally this was an exercise for his own use, but he published sections of his translation a few years later. Yet, while respecting the military teachings of Potsdam and Berlin, he deplored the patronizing arrogance of the foreign instructors; they must, he argued among his friends, recognize that there was a Turkish national identity distinct from the Islamic virtues which the Kaiser so admired. Privately in the staff college Kemal, Ali Fuad and other young officers began to wonder, as had many of their predecessors over the past half-century, if the sultanate with its claim to imperial sovereignty did not stifle Turkish national consciousness rather than promote it.

In the second week of January 1905 Kemal passed out as a staff captain, fifth in a class of fifty-seven. While awaiting a posting he lodged in the Beyazit district. There he and his friends talked too rashly for their good. A police spy denounced them and they spent several weeks in the prison cells, uncertain of their fate. Eventually they were treated leniently. It was decided that Kemal and Ali Fuad were too dangerous to remain in the capital; better for them to practise soldiering with the Fifth Army in distant Syria. So primitive were communications around the Turkish coast that it took them two months to sail from the Bosphorus to Beirut.[5]

Most of the next two years Kemal spent at Damascus. The inefficiency and corruption of the Fifth Army appalled him and he was surprised to find traditional Muslim beliefs imposing social restraints which had begun to lapse in European Turkey. He was soon separated from Ali Fuad, who went on a mission to Sheikh Ibn Saud at Riyadh, a primitive walled town around an oasis

14

in the centre of the Arabian desert. But Kemal found other educated Turks in Damascus willing to join him in a nationalistic secret society. *Vatan* – the Fatherland Movement – was founded in Damascus in October 1906 and soon afterwards Kemal established cells in Jaffa, Jerusalem and Beirut.[6] But he had greater ambitions. Secretly he travelled to Alexandria, and took a ship to Piraeus where he was able to find a coastal vessel sailing north to his native Salonika. There he spent some weeks with his mother – now widowed for a second time – and his sister. He was beginning to build a network of *Vatan* groups around Salonika when he was warned that police reports about him had been sent to Constantinople. With remarkable speed he returned to Syria, immersing himself so completely in his studies, that the slow and bungling authorities in the capital assumed that their police spy had made a mistake; it must have been some other Mustafa who had been seen at Salonika.

This secret visit home convinced Kemal that if he was to influence his country's political life he needed to be in European Turkey rather than the Levant. To his great satisfaction he secured a posting to Salonika in September 1907. But he found that the *Vatan* cells established in the previous autumn were dormant. Other young radical officers in the garrison towns of Turkish Macedonia had set up a conspiratorial network which soon became known as the Committee of Union and Progress (CUP). With some reluctance Kemal agreed that his *Vatan* movement should affiliate with the larger organization; he mistrusted the CUP leaders, and he deplored the way in which they looked for inspiration to the teachings of the mullahs. His experiences in Syria had convinced him that Turkey could never be modernized so long as Muslim institutions dominated Ottoman society. He had insisted that *Vatan* members should pledge their loyalty to the fatherland on a revolver: CUP initiates swore an oath on the traditional symbols of militant Islam, the sword and the Koran.[7]

At midsummer 1908 a rebellion broke out in Turkish Macedonia, originally in units of the Third Army around Ochrid and Monastir. Kemal, who was acting as military inspector of guard-posts along the railway up the Vardar to Üsküb (now known as Skopje), played no part in the revolt, which seems to have taken him by surprise. The initiative was seized by Kemal's contemporary, Major Enver, an early member of CUP. Enver sensed that the conspirators had a greater chance of attaining a direct objective than of winning wide support for a vague and ambitious programme of major reforms. The CUP accordingly demanded, quite simply, that Sultan Abdul Hamid should restore the parliamentary constitution which he had accepted in December 1876 and suspended fifteen months later. At first Abdul Hamid underestimated the danger up in the remote mountains of his empire's northwest frontier. Troops from Anatolia were sent against the rebellious Third Army. To the Sultan's consternation their officers joined the insurgents. On 23 July 1908 Abdul Hamid capitulated. After thirty years of despotic rule, he agreed to bring the constitution of 1876 out of cold storage; the Ottoman Empire would have an elected parliament.

There was widespread rejoicing in Constantinople and the provincial cities of European Turkey. The Young Turks, as the CUP leaders were called, had achieved an almost bloodless triumph. In Salonika Major Enver, a dapper officer liberally endowed with charismatic glamour, became a popular idol overnight. When he appeared on the balcony of the Olympos Palace Hotel, Kemal was there, standing somewhere in the background; but no one doubted that it was Enver's day. As Kemal's own friends later admitted, he was deeply jealous of Enver's sudden emergence from obscurity.[8]

Elections for an assembly of 280 deputies took place in the autumn, and in the closing days of the year the sixty-

six-year-old Sultan personally opened parliament. But by
the following spring a reaction set in. The deputies were
beginning to propose reforms which threatened Islamic
supremacy in the Empire. On 13 April 1909 students from
the religious schools in the capital, backed by fundamentalists of an older generation, led a protest movement; demonstrators burst into the parliament chamber,
assassinated two deputies and began to call for ven-
geance on the godless Young Turks. Abdul Hamid
encouraged the counter-revolution, which was backed by
the First Army, garrisoning the capital itself. The headquarters of CUP was still in Salonika. Kemal, who had
been sent by the Young Turks on a mission to Tripoli and
Benghazi, was back in his birthplace and, at the news of
the counter-revolution, he conferred with the senior
officers; Enver, who was in Berlin as military attaché,
hurried down to Salonika. It was resolved that the Third
Army would march on Constantinople from Macedonia.
The advance would be led by General Mahmud Shevket,
with Kemal as his chief-of-staff. Civil war seemed
imminent.

Mahmud Shevket and Kemal reached San Stefano, at
the approaches to the capital, on the evening of 24 April.
There was little opposition in the city, apart from areas
around two barracks. Two days later Abdul Hamid was
under virtual house arrest at Yildiz. There a deputation
brought him a *Fetva* (a religious decree of deposition),
which made him surrender the sultanate to his sixty-four-
year-old brother who, after more than half a century of
virtual imprisonment, acceded as Sultan Mehmed V.
Abdul Hamid, to his great indignation, was put aboard a
special train before dawn on 28 April and exiled to Salonika, the city where his troubles had begun. Thirteen of
his thirty-three predecessors had been deposed, the
majority dying mysteriously within a few weeks or
months. Abdul Hamid, however, was to survive another
nine years, ending his days in a Bosphorus palace after

17

the Turks were ejected from Macedonia.[9]

Throughout the first year of Mehmed V's reign Salonika remained the power-house of the Young Turk movement. A CUP Congress met there in July 1909 at which Kemal made his earliest known political speech, as delegate for Tripolitania. He showed himself far more critical of the Young Turk leadership than most CUP members, arguing that serving officers should resign from the army if they wished to play an active role in party politics. Gradually Kemal gathered a nucleus of dissidents around him: old friends such as Ali Fethi and Ali Fuad, and newcomers whom he first met at San Stefano: Rauf, an Anglophile naval officer; Ismet, the gunnery specialist from the Adrianople garrison; and Kiazim, one of Mahmud Shevket's staff officers. This group formed a radical, nationalist wing within the CUP. They remained hostile to the ruling triumvirate of Young Turks, all of whom Kemal had encountered during 1908 in Salonika: Jemal; Talaat; and above all Enver, whom he already regarded as an arch-rival.

Kemal, true to the arguments he presented at the Salonika Congress, resolved to eschew active politics and concentrate on his military duties. Briefly he was commander of an infantry regiment; he then once again served Mahmud Shevket as chief-of-staff, planning a brilliantly executed operation to forestall a major insurrection in Albania. But he continued to widen his horizons. In 1910 Kemal joined his friend Fethi (who was serving as military attaché in Paris) for the French manoeuvres in Picardy. Yet, although Kemal was fascinated by all that he saw of Western ways in France, he was still too gauche – and too junior among the Young Turks – to score a social success. In the autumn of 1909 Enver had attended German army manoeuvres near Würzburg, where he had made a deep impression on a fellow guest, Winston Churchill; in February 1910 Enver came to London, where his polished courtesies charmed more than one political hostess. No flattering invitations followed Kemal's field days in Picardy.[10]

In September 1911 Kemal took up a staff post in Constantinople. He had been there only a fortnight when Italy declared war on Turkey, complaining of maltreatment of Italian traders in the Sultan's last two remaining provinces (*vilayets*) in North Africa: Tripolitania and Benghazi. The Italian fleet bombarded the coast and landed troops near Tripoli, the city Kemal had represented at the Salonika Congress. Enver and his personal staff hurriedly travelled in mufti to Libya across British-administered Egypt. Kemal, with two companions, followed Enver's example a few days later, only to find the British authorities on the alert and rigidly neutral. Somewhere between Sollum and Bardia the Turkish officers, by then in uniform, met a British patrol whose leader was persuaded by Kemal into believing that he had strayed across the frontier. Soon afterwards Kemal's party reached the Turkish lines outside Tobruk, which was already in Italian hands.

Kemal spent some ten months campaigning in Cyrenaica during this largely forgotten Libyan War, for much of the summer of 1912 serving alongside Enver near Derna.[11] In retrospect it is clear that the Young Turks overstretched the Ottoman Empire's resources in their determination to defend provinces which had been for many years financial losses. The Turkish army seemed so ill-prepared for war that the Balkan States felt encouraged to come together in an alliance aimed at expelling the Turks for all time from Europe. Kiamal Pasha, who as Grand Vizier was effective head of the Ottoman government, was as surprised by the coming of the Balkan Wars in October 1912 as by the Italian attack thirteen months before. Because of Ottoman commitments in North Africa and in southern Arabia (where the tribesmen of the Hejaz and Yemen were in revolt), the Turkish field armies in Europe were outnumbered by more than two to one –

the Balkan allies (Serbia, Greece, Bulgaria, Montenegro) could put 715,000 troops into the field; the Turks, at the most, 325,000 men. Seven days after the outbreak of this new war, Turkey concluded a preliminary peace with Italy at Ouchy; the final treaty deprived the Ottoman Empire of its two Libyan provinces and the islands of the Dodecanese as well.

Had Turkey's ablest young officers been content in 1911 to remain at Constantinople or in its hinterland, the Balkan allies would not have gained the rapid succession of victories which so nearly lost the Ottomans their foothold in Europe. The war played havoc with Ottoman communications. If it had been difficult to reach Tobruk in the previous winter, it was even harder to find a speedy route back to the new Balkan Front. Kemal had only reached Cairo when he heard that his native Salonika was in Greek hands and that the Serbs held the two familiar garrison towns of Monastir and Üsküb. To return to Constantinople that winter he had to take a ship to either an Italian port or (more probably) Marseilles, and then travel in a succession of trains through Austria, Hungary and Romania in order to board a Black Sea steamer at Constanza. When he landed at Galata in mid-November, the Bulgarian army was attacking the Chatalja defences, barely twenty miles from the walls of the capital.

Zubeyde, now aged about sixty, had been forced to flee from Salonika, together with her daughter Makbule and two nieces of her second husband, Fikriye and Julide. Kemal found his mother and her frightened companions among the refugees in Constantinople, who clustered pathetically in the courtyards of mosques during the heavy rainstorms which seemed to continue day after day that winter.[12] After renting a house in Pera for Zubeyde and her family, Kemal began to plan operations to relieve the Turkish garrison encircled at Adrianople (now known as Edirne). But with the first snow sweeping westwards from Anatolia, such planning became a largely academic exercise; the weather was so grim that it took seven hours for an order from divisional headquarters to reach the sodden trenches around Chatalja. The Turks and Bulgarians agreed on a ceasefire on 3 December.

The military disasters of the year 1912 in North Africa and the Balkans were an indictment of CUP policies. A decree on military training issued four months after Abdul Hamid's deposition had caused confusion in the more distant garrisons of the Ottoman Empire. Many modern weapons purchased from the Germans proved too sophisticated for use by troops unfamiliar with the techniques of Western armies. But Enver, on returning from Derna, was eager to put the blame elsewhere: it was, he insisted, the fault of the war minister, Nazim Pasha. On 23 January 1913 Enver personally led a mob into the principal office of Ottoman government, the council chamber of the Sublime Porte. One of his companions shot Nazim dead, while Enver secured the resignation of Kiamal Pasha. The Sultan, a total nonentity, agreed to appoint Mahmud Shevket as his new Grand Vizier. But from now onwards the real master of Turkey was Colonel Enver Pasha.[13]

Kemal deplored Enver's *coup d'état* but welcomed the appointment of Shevket. There remained, however, little time for politics. Fighting broke out again around Adrianople in the first week of February and it proved impossible to relieve the garrison. The city fell to the Bulgarians on 26 March. In revenge for this humiliation and for the murder of Nazim, a hit-squad of assassins killed Shevket as he was driving in a car through the narrow streets of the Beyazit district. Although some officers hostile to the Young Turks were hurriedly court-martialled and hanged, it was rumoured that Enver had connived at the conspiracy as he wanted a more malleable Grand Vizier. Shevket's successor, Prince Said Halim, was a well-meaning elderly gentleman, disinclined to quarrel with any popular hero. It only remained for Enver to ensure that he was himself cast in that particular role.

At the end of June 1913 the Bulgarians gave Enver the opportunity for which he had hoped: they quarrelled with their allies over the spoils of war and were themselves so locked in battle with their neighbours that they had to withdraw troops from the Turkish border. Kemal's plans for the relief of Adrianople were belatedly put into action. Steadily the Turkish army advanced westwards until it became clear that Adrianople could be recovered without another long siege. As the Turks were about to enter the city, Enver led a cavalry detachment which galloped ahead of the marching columns. This action, infuriating to Kemal and his brother officers, made Enver the hero of Adrianople. As a good Muslim, who also carried a copy of the Koran in his tunic pocket, he knew what was expected of him. It was reported that he went at once to the great Selimye Mosque to offer his prayers to Allah.

The Balkan Wars were a traumatic experience for thousands of people living in Constantinople during the winter of 1913–14: many had lost homes in cities where their families had lived for generations; all had heard the thud of shells as the enemy pounded the Chatalja lines, the last defences outside the capital. Fear and disillusionment made them look for a hero-protector; after the recovery of Adrianople, they believed they had found one in Colonel Enver. It was not until the beginning of 1914 that he held high office – Minister of War – but his style of leadership made him behave as if he was already the Bonaparte of the Bosphorus. He was married to Princess Emine Naciye, the fourteen-year-old granddaughter of Sultan Abdul Mejid I; she bore him children at their delightful home in one of the smaller waterfront palaces. His ambitions, too, matched those of the young Napoleon. He believed that the Ottoman Empire must look again to its Asian origins while retaining a firm foothold in Europe; he was attracted by the Pan-Turanian movement, which sought to restore the Sultan's authority in the Caucasus and beyond, perhaps even encompassing the old Mogul lands of India. All this was anathema to Kemal, with his westernized and nationalistic outlook. Enver's links with the ruling House, his strict religious observance and his assumption that there was a role for a revitalized Ottoman dynasty in the twentieth century seemed to run counter to the original plans of the CUP. Briefly Kemal hoped to curb Enver's incipient Bonapartism by reviving the CUP, with Fethi as its secretary in place of Talaat.

Almost certainly, had the roles been reversed, an all-powerful Kemal would have sent a dissident Enver and his followers to the gallows. But the triumvirate did not wish to open fresh rifts in the Young Turk movement. A new – and as yet top secret – German military mission was, so Enver hoped, about to lick the Turkish Army into shape again after the humiliations of the past year. Fethi, it was decided, should go to Bulgaria as Turkey's minister (ambassador), taking his friend Lieutenant-Colonel Kemal with him as military attaché. Both potential trouble-makers would therefore be in honourable exile before the arrival in Constantinople of the German military mission. Kemal received his appointment to Sofia on 27 October. On the following day in Berlin General Liman von Sanders signed with Turkish representatives a treaty, approved by Kaiser Wilhelm II, which provided for the progressive 'Germanization of the Turkish army'.[14]

Exile in Sofia was an agreeable experience. Kemal liked the theatres and the opera, the cafés and the westernized dress for men and women; he enjoyed in particular the company of the minister of war's daughter, Dimitriana Kovachev. At one time he considered resigning from the Turkish army, marrying 'Miti', and becoming a teacher, for he had always felt a desire to implant new ideas in others. Fethi, too, wished to marry a Bulgarian general's daughter.

But, although King Ferdinand and his High Command theoretically favoured reconciliation with the Turkish enemy, the prospect of having Fethi and Kemal as sons-in-law strained the patriotism of even the most loyal of Bulgarian officers; two stern fathers duly cut short their daughters' romances. For Kemal the chief consequences of his evenings with Miti in Sofia were an opinion that a modern capital city needs an opera house (Ankara was to get one in 1927) and a conviction that Turkish men would feel liberated from reactionary influences if only they wore hats instead of the fez. Such a sacrilegious sartorial revolution would never have appealed to Enver.[15]

Although Kemal enjoyed the social life of Sofia, there seemed to him to be no firm basis for an understanding between Bulgaria and her Ottoman neighbour. Two and a half weeks after the Sarajevo assassination, when war clouds loomed over central Europe, Kemal sent a strongly worded report to Enver warning him that Bulgaria would almost certainly fight on the side of Austria–Hungary in any major European conflict on the understanding that Bulgaria would then become the dominant power in the Balkans. Kemal opposed a German alliance for the Turks: he believed that if Germany won a European war, the Ottoman Empire would survive only as a political and economic dependency of Prussia; if Germany lost, the Ottoman Empire would be partitioned among the victors. These arguments made no impression on Enver. When World War I broke out in August 1914 there were already almost a hundred German officers serving in Liman von Sander's military mission, a figure which soon multiplied five times over. Liman was himself commanding general of the Turkish army group defending Constantinople.

In Sofia Kemal had mounting evidence of the German infiltration of his homeland. During the last week of August ninety German naval officers and specialized personnel passed through the Bulgarian capital on their way to Constantinople, where the German battle-cruiser *Goeben* and light cruiser *Breslau* had taken refuge from a British squadron in the second week of August. A month later the German admiral, Wilhelm Souchon, was appointed commander-in-chief of the Turkish fleet: the *Goeben* became the Turkish flagship and was renamed *Jawuz Sultan Selim*; the *Breslau* was renamed *Midelli*. Turkish entry into the war as an ally of Germany and Austria–Hungary by now seemed inevitable. At the end of October Admiral Souchon's squadron bombarded the Russian Black Sea coast; within a few days Russia, Great Britain, France and Serbia declared war on Turkey.

Although Kemal deplored the drift into the Great Power conflict he sought an immediate posting to the war zone rather than remain in neutral Sofia. Enver, as War Minister, at first proposed that he should organize a small expedition which would cross Persia and raise Muslim India in revolt against the British Raj. Kemal regarded this project as yet another manifestation of Enver's Napoleonic fantasy and refused the command. But when Enver was away from the capital, at the Caucasian front, Kemal returned to Constantinople and asked the Deputy War Minister for a field command. After days of muddle and prevarication he was appointed to a newly formed XIXth Division attached to General Liman von Sanders's Fifth Army, which was responsible for the land defences of the Dardanelles. On 25 February 1915 Kemal set up his headquarters in Maidos, at the neck of the Gallipoli peninsula.

Gallipoli and After $\quad$ 2

The Gallipoli peninsula curves like an elegant forefinger
over the Dardanelles, the thirty-three-mile waterway
which through the centuries has linked the rulers of
Constantinople with the Mediterranean world. Across the
Straits, like a stubby thumb to Gallipoli's finger, lies the
Asiatic shore, less than a mile across at Çanakkale
(formerly Chanak) on the narrows and only four miles at
the south-western tip of Cape Helles, where Byron once
swam to the ancient coast of Troy. The forts commanding the Dardanelles were therefore key defences for the
Ottoman Empire, protecting the approaches to the
capital, 120 miles to the east. Their strategic importance
had already been recognized by the Sultan's enemies:
during the Libyan War Italian warships exchanged fire
with shore batteries for a few hours in April 1912; and on
3 November 1914 – two days before the declaration of
war on Turkey – British and French battleships
bombarded the outer forts on either side of the
Dardanelles. By the end of February 1915, when Kemal
arrived at Maidos, General Liman von Sanders had
concentrated six divisions (84,000 men) on the European
and Asian shores of the Straits. The forts commanding

the waterway bristled with Krupp guns.

Even so, Liman von Sanders was apprehensive. The guns were too old, he complained; some of the stone-work of the forts was medieval; and there were no trenches on the dominant heights which could form the basis of a defence system if the enemy established a bridgehead after landing in force. As for the Turkish officers, he thought little of the ruling clique whom he had met, from Enver downwards. However, he acknow-ledged the soldierly qualities of the elderly General Essad Pasha, the 'knightly and valorous' commander of the Third Army Corps, who was responsible for the sector from the town of Gallipoli (now known as Gelibolu) down to Maidos. Soon, too, Liman came to respect Colonel Mustafa Kemal, although the German's memoirs show that he always found him an exasperating companion in arms.[1]

Kemal was well established on the peninsula by 18 March 1915, when he saw for himself the failure of the principal naval assault on the Dardanelles: one in three of the British and French capital ships was sunk or incapaci-tated that day. He became convinced that, since it was impossible for Entente seapower to force a passage up the Dardanelles, the enemy would soon mount an invasion; he assumed that troops would land under cover of heavy bombardment from warships out at sea, beyond the range of the coastal forts. Assaults of this character were familiar to him from the Libyan War; he knew that the best counter-measures depended on bringing reinforcements speedily to threatened sectors of the Front. He was therefore content to keep his division as a mobile reserve with headquarters at Boghali, on the heights four miles above Maidos, a position which would enable him to concentrate his men to counter an attack on the peninsula itself or to ferry reserves across to Chanak so as to check an incursion on the Asiatic shore. Liman believed the landings would be made north of the peninsula around Bulair in order to sever the isthmus, and on the Trojan littoral; Kemal was certain that they would come on the Gallipoli peninsula itself. He thought the most likely places were around Cape Helles, where naval guns could give maximum support, and at Gabe Tepe on the Aegean coast, where there were no Turkish forts and a relatively short route for any invader to advance across the peninsula and reach the narrows. He was right.

Almost every day during that spring of 1915 Kemal kept the XIXth Division on the alert with training exercises on the hills around Boghali. His own account of events makes vivid reading. He was preparing for yet another field day on 25 April when he heard a heavy bombardment by naval guns. The shells seemed to be falling north-east of Gabe Tepe, where he had expected the landing, some four miles across the main ridge of the peninsula. He sent out a cavalry squadron and prepared to follow it with an infantry regiment and a mountain battery. It was a precipitous climb to the summit of Koja Cemen Tepe, at 971 feet the highest point on the peninsula. From there Kemal and a small group of officers went forward on foot through rough scrubland to a smaller promontory, Chunuk Bair, reaching this vantage point well ahead of the main body of their men. At first Kemal could see the warships firing out at sea, but not the invaders themselves. A strong current had carried them north of Gabe Tepe to an isolated beach which the Turks called Ari Burnu, the 'Bees' Cove'. Henceforth it was to be known as 'Anzac Cove', thus perpetuating the memory of the Australian and New Zealand Army Corps who waded ashore at daybreak that Sunday.

To his dismay Kemal saw, not an advancing enemy, but a detachment of Turkish soldiers in full flight through the scrub. His own account reads: 'Confronting the fugitives, I shouted to them, "What is the matter? Why are you running away?" "They come, they come, sir, the enemy – English, English."' They pointed wildly across the scrubland, where Kemal's field glasses focused on an Australasian advance party who were by now nearer to him than the men of his own division. '"You cannot run away from the enemy," I shouted to the fugitives. "We have no ammunition," they said. "If you have no ammunition, you still have your bayonets," I replied. I made them fix bayonets and lie down on the ground ... As our men lay down, so the enemy lay down too. This gave us the pause in time which we needed to gain.' The Turkish 57th Regiment took up defensive positions, the mountain battery fired shrapnel to check the Anzacs, more troops were summoned from Maidos, and the impulse of the invasion was gone for all time.[2]

Kemal possessed the magnetic personality which turned waverers into heroes. It was on this occasion that he issued his most famous battle order: 'I am not ordering you to attack; I am ordering you to die. In the time that it takes us to die other troops can come up and take our places.' This terrible fervour sustained the defence throughout that first morning of battle – and the 57th Regiment was almost wiped out. But the invaders could make little progress. The error by which the Anzacs had landed on the wrong beach meant that they were concentrated on a narrow front from which it was difficult to penetrate inland. Turkish artillery inflicted heavy casualties upon them, forcing them back by nightfall to the outcrops of rock above the beaches where they had scrambled ashore. For six days and nights Kemal threw more and more troops against the invaders, failing to dislodge them. 'I cannot believe that there is anyone in the troops I command who would not die rather than suffer again the disgrace that fell upon us in the Balkans,' he declared in another rousing order of the day.[3] A third major onslaught brought retribution from the British warships, their shells landing on Kemal's improvised trench system. He threw his last reserves into a night attack after a day of exhaustion; but still he could not dislodge the Anzac enemy. These were the actions of a fanatic rather than the rationalized tactics of a trained staff officer; and a week after the battle began, General Essad persuaded Kemal to waste no more men on such desperate attacks.

On two occasions – in mid-May and early June – Enver personally ordered the Turks to take the offensive and try, yet again, to clear Anzac Cove in order to lift the threat to the vulnerable central sector. Each attack came to grief against the carefully constructed Anzac dugouts, for by now Gallipoli was as criss-crossed by trenches as any salient on the Western Front. It seemed unlikely, however, that the allied commanders would settle for a war of attrition, as was the case in France and Flanders, and Kemal began to speculate on the intentions of Turkey's enemies. He had correctly forecast where the invaders would land; now he sought to convince his German and Turkish senior officers that the British would use Anzac Cove and its neighbouring beaches as a springboard for their assault on the heights of the central ridge. Liman von Sanders was impressed, but Essad and the other divisional commanders thought it impossible for the enemy to mount an offensive in such a rugged and arid terrain without substantial reinforcements of men and material.

Once again Kemal was right, at least geographically. The British Xth and XIth Divisions landed at Suvla Bay on the night of 6–7 August and soon made contact with the Anzacs, immediately to their south. Neither Essad nor Kemal had reckoned on a night offensive, and Turkish intelligence failed to detect the build-up in Anzac's own strength over the previous nights. The initiative was once more with the British and Australasians. If they could dislodge the Turks from the ridge of Sari Bair and the Anafarta Hills to the north of it, victory would be theirs. The Turks on the Cape Helles Front would be cut off;

minesweepers could clear a path for warships up the Dardanelles without artillery bombardment from the European shore. Faced with such a threat from the Suvla landing, Liman von Sanders acted decisively. As Kemal had shown that he could anticipate the enemy's intentions, during the night of 8–9 August Liman appointed him commander of all the troops in the Anafarta Hills. His orders were to stop the invaders' advance before the Gallipoli peninsula was cut in two. It was a great responsibility for a thirty-four-year-old officer who had been accorded the rank of full colonel only two months before.

'Mustafa Kemal of Anafarta' was soon to become a hero respected by his fellow countrymen and their German ally; name and place were readily associated with each other, much as Lord Roberts and Kandahar or Lord Kitchener and Khartoum had been in late Victorian Britain. He allowed none of his subordinates to rest, visiting each position in the hills repeatedly and – according to one eye-witness – leading a bayonet charge in person when weary troops wavered. Thursday, 10 August, was the critical moment in the battle. On that day Kemal decided to make a frontal attack at dawn on Chunuk Bair, a hilltop on the Sari Bair ridge which a small group of British troops had seized. Wave after wave of Turkish troops went forward until by midday, Chunuk Bair was recovered. Kemal himself scorned death. A young officer saw him suddenly give a convulsive start. 'Sir, you are hit,' he exclaimed; only to be told: 'Keep silent.' A piece of shrapnel had hit Kemal over the heart, but the impact was absorbed by a watch which he carried in his breast pocket. It left, so he wrote later, 'a rather big pool of blood', but he insisted on remaining in the front line until the fighting died away. That night Kemal reported his victory in person to Liman von Sanders and dramatically presented the German general with his shattered watch. Both men recognized that the assault on the hills had been checked. A few miles away, at Allied GHQ, Captain Compton Mackenzie wrote in his diary that evening: 'Feeling pretty rotten ... I see no chance of standing a winter campaign and no chance of forcing the Dardanelles before winter.'[4]

Fourteen years later Brigadier-General Aspinall-Oglander, a staff officer who had landed at Suvla that week, completed the British official history, *Military Operations, Gallipoli*, with a considered judgement on Kemal's fighting qualities in the peninsula: 'Seldom in history can the exertions of a single divisional commander have exercised ... so profound an influence not only on the course of a battle but, perhaps, on the fate of a campaign and even the destiny of a nation.'[5] It was a verdict with which the divisional commander himself warmly concurred, for Kemal, for whom modesty and self-deprecation always held as little attraction as for Napoleon, believed even in the autumn of 1915 that he deserved to be fêted as Turkey's saviour. In this he was disappointed. His officers and men respected and trusted him, but he could not overcome the hostility of Enver and his colleagues in the ruling triumvirate, Mehmed Talaat and Ahmed Djemal. When the official magazine of the Turkish war ministry wished to display Kemal's portrait on the cover of an issue celebrating his victory, Enver personally intervened: there was to be no triumphal trumpeting of Colonel Kemal's achievements. The feud between Enver and Kemal intensified as the war years posed new problems of policy; genuine differences of principle were heightened by an unsophisticated mutual jealousy.

All that summer Kemal's health was poor. He was racked by bouts of malaria and weak from the chronic kidney trouble which was to plague him in later years. In the closing days of December he was granted sick leave and returned to Constantinople. No hero's welcome awaited him; he was not, as he had hoped, made a general nor was he given the courtesy title of Pasha.

When, ten days after his arrival in Constantinople, news came that the Allies had evacuated the Gallipoli peninsula, he was living quietly with his mother and sister on the coastal road at Besiktas, between the Sultan's palaces at Dolmabahçe and Yildiz. Soon he found accommodation in the Pera Palace Hotel, partly to escape Zubeyde's well-intentioned ministrations but also to keep in closer contact with political life. He frequently criticized Enver's dependence on the Germans in conversations with his friend Hussein Rauf, the distinguished naval officer, then serving in the Ministry of Marine. Kemal found time, too, to enjoy the company of an attractive cabaret artiste, to travel to Sofia and renew old friendships, and to start a long love affair with his kinswoman, Fikriye.[6]

Although Kemal had left Gallipoli quietly enough, he made certain he would return to active service in a blaze of glory. On being given command of the Sixteenth Army Corps, he transferred from the peninsula to Adrianople, he insisted that the corps and its commander should enter the city as a victorious army returning from the wars. No doubt it was good for the morale of the Sixteenth Army Corps and heartening for the people of Adrianople, but news of the victory parade made galling reading for Enver, whose own military reputation had been built on the recovery of that city from the Bulgarians at the end of the Balkan Wars. Within six weeks both Kemal and his troops received a new posting, out to south-eastern Turkey to stem the advance of the Russians, who had already captured Erzurum and the port of Trabzon. Kemal's headquarters were at Diyarbakir, in the summer months a baking oven of a walled city whose medieval watch-towers looked out across the upper Tigris to a dust-bowl, the Sanhurfa desert. Diyarbakir was 860 miles from the Bosphorus and – of more immediate military significance – over 500 miles from the nearest railhead, at Konya. To compensate Kemal for such an unpromising command, he was informed, soon after setting out for the East, that he had been promoted to general and accorded the title of Pasha.

The front line was more than a hundred miles east of Diyarbakir, around Lake Van. There, in the first week of August 1916, Kemal gained a victory against the Russians, capturing the hill town of Bitlis. Back in Diyarbakir, where the winters were as bleak as the summers were hot, he was given command of the Second Army and began to plan a spring offensive against the war-weary Russians. In those winter months of 1916–17 he was served as chief-of-staff by Colonel Ismet. The two men had known each other in 1909, during the march to quell Abdul Hamid's counter-revolution, but it was at Diyarbakir that their collaboration began in earnest. Ismet was an admirable partner, efficient and more cautious than Kemal, critics sometimes complaining that he was unimaginative. But their plans that winter were never executed. Revolution at home pulled the Russians back from Turkish Kurdistan.

Early in July 1917 Kemal was appointed to command a newly constituted Seventh Army, based at Aleppo. He assumed that he was to train the troops and bring them into action in Palestine. To his surprise he discovered that the Seventh Army would be the key unit in Army Group *Yildirim* ('Lightning'), a force intended by Enver to move quickly across northern Syria and into Mesopotamia, where it was to recapture Baghdad from the British, press forward into Persia and force the Entente Powers into a major revision of general strategy by threatening India. Kemal thought this project absurd; it was a recipe for disaster since there was no hope of keeping *Yildirim* supplied as it thrust deeper and deeper into central Asia.

Nor was this strategy Kemal's only grievance. He was furious to discover that in Army Group *Yildirim* he would be subordinate to another newly imported eminent Prussian, Field Marshal Erich von Falkenhayn, who had been

Chief of the Greater German General Staff until the
ghastly failure at Verdun destroyed his credibility. Kemal
found it hard to believe that Falkenhayn would support
so rash an enterprise as the proposed march on Baghdad. When he met him at Aleppo he made no attempt to
conceal his hostility. Although Falkenhayn continued to
regard Kemal as a mutinous subordinate, he gradually
came to recognize the defects in the *Yildirim* masterplan.

By early September Falkenhayn had decided against it.
He now favoured an alternative project, dear to Enver's
heart: the 'lightning' blow would fall in Palestine, with a
massive thrust through Sinai which would carry the
Turkish Seventh Army and a German Asia Corps from
Gaza across the Suez Canal and into Egypt. But Kemal
thought that this proposal, too, was courting disaster.
One of Falkenhayn's closest advisers was Major von
Papen, who became German chancellor and ambassador
in Ankara during World War II. Papen recalls in his
memoirs how he met General Mustafa Kemal Pasha at 'a
water-hole in the hills south of Hebron' during September
1917 and found him 'in a fearful temper' having 'had a
serious misunderstanding with Falkenhayn.'[7] Their differences ran deeper than Papen realized: Kemal had
recently drafted a long report to Enver on corruption and
chaos in the Turkish administration of Syria, inade-
quacies in the troops sent out to him from Constantinople, and the need for a major change in policy which
would assert the independence of the Turkish army
rather than allow it to continue as a work-horse serving
German imperial ambitions. Some of his criticisms were
detailed and staggering: he had, for example, found the
men so physically weak in one of his divisions that half of
them could not even stand on parade, let alone march
against the enemy. Unless drastic changes were made in
the composition of the Seventh Army, the administration
of Syria and the relationship between the Turks and the
six thousand newly despatched specialists of the German

Asia Corps, Kemal informed Enver, he would be forced to resign his command.[8]

Kemal's report caused a sensation at Constantinople, even though it was circulated among only a few leading figures. The War Ministry cannot have been surprised to learn of the poor quality of the men whom it had drafted into the Seventh Army. More significant were the report's political implications. For it was clear that Falkenhayn's assumption of supreme command in the Levant had been resented, not only by Kemal, but by one of the Young Turks triumvirate, General Ahmed Djemal, who had led a force of 20,000 men across the centre of the Sinai desert in January 1915 and taken the British by surprise on the Suez Canal. Djemal was still the senior Turkish general on the Palestine Front and understood the problems of the terrain and climate far better than any German outsider. If hostility to Falkenhayn had brought Kemal and Djemal together in a political alliance, then Enver risked isolation and personal defeat as the sole champion of a German alliance in the Sultan's government. Enver accordingly hurried down to Damascus for talks with Kemal, Djemal and Falkenhayn. He found the two Turks angered by Falkenhayn's arrogant manner but mutually suspicious of each other. It seemed unlikely they would remain long in collaboration. Kemal, however, remained implacably hostile towards every proposal put forward by Falkenhayn and no smooth words from the Minister of War could mollify him. Enver urged Kemal to go once more to Diyarbakir and lead the Second Army into the Caucasus, but he refused to accept the new appointment. He was determined to return to the centre of affairs.

Enver wished to avoid a political crisis. Rather than allow Kemal to resign his command, he proposed that he should take a month's leave. But the war ministry had no intention of helping a near-mutinous commander to return to Constantinople. Kemal had to sell his horses to Djemal in order to raise money for the train fare to

Aleppo and across Anatolia to the Haydarpasa Station at Scutari on the Asian shore of the Bosphorus. When, in mid-October, he reached Haydarpasa he found the station a scene of desolation, for five weeks previously the whole of Scutari had been shaken by a massive explosion. British agents had fired an ammunition dump, destroying in one huge flash, ordnance and supplies intended for the Seventh Army and the German Asia Corps. Most of the German specialists were still stranded at Haydarpasa when Kemal stepped down from his train.[9]

Once back in Constantinople Kemal could rely on finding attentive listeners to his catalogue of grievances. As well as Rauf at the Ministry of Marine, there was his old friend from the Monastir Military School, Ali Fethi, now a parliamentary deputy. Both men recognized the gravity of Kemal's complaints. When, in the first days of November, news came of Allenby's surprise offensive at Beersheba, Kemal's friends feared the worst. The British took Gaza on 9 November and Jaffa eight days later. Early in December the Turkish resistance outside Jerusalem crumbled away, exposing all the weaknesses which Kemal had perceived. By Christmas the Holy City was held securely in British hands.

The magnitude of these defeats made Rauf believe that the Turkish army needed an active Kemal serving once again in the field. He had used his considerable diplomatic tact to bring Enver and Kemal together late in November, before Allenby's offensive had reached Jerusalem: they were his luncheon guests in the Pera Palace Hotel. At first Enver encouraged Kemal to give up the army and join Fethi as a politician; but Kemal knew that his great bargaining power was his military reputation. He remained Turkey's undefeated general, and he had no intention of entering politics at such a critical moment in the war. Enver, however, was by now staking everything on increased German support; he believed that with both revolutionary Russia and Romania seeking a separate peace, the Germans would have men and material to spare in the East. He therefore could not risk giving the anti-German Kemal another field command. It would be better if he could learn to love the Germans. To Kemal's surprise, soon after the luncheon at the Pera Palace, he was appointed principal military aide-de-camp to the Sultan's heir apparent, Prince Vahideddin, who was about to visit Germany as a guest of Kaiser Wilhelm II.

Vahideddin was a fifty-six-year-old nonentity, with no experience of politics and little understanding of war. At their first meeting Kemal was unimpressed; the Prince had a thin figure, with drooping shoulders, drooping eyelids and a drooping manner. But as their train crawled northwards through Bulgaria on the long journey to German headquarters, the Prince sent for Kemal and flattered him; had he not saved the capital by his courage and enterprise at Gallipoli? The flattery continued when the visitors reached their destination: 'Sixteenth Army Corps! Anafarta!' Wilhelm II barked out confidently by way of greeting. The Kaiser was always well briefed on such occasions – as Kemal, with his experience of court life at Sofia, cynically suspected.

At German GHQ the Turkish visitors were received by Field Marshal von Hindenburg and his deputy, General Ludendorff; this formidable partnership failed to overawe Kemal. When he heard Hindenburg giving the Prince an optimistic analysis of reports from the Syrian Front, Kemal decided that the field marshal was bluffing; and he was not impressed by Hindenburg's reluctance to explain the objectives of the new German offensive in the West. That night, after a champagne banquet given by the Kaiser, Kemal turned directly to Hindenburg: 'Your Excellency,' he said, 'the facts which you gave this morning to Prince Vahideddin about the Syrian Front were quite wrong. I know; I was there; the cavalry division you mentioned exists only on paper. But we will let that pass. However, as a favour, would you tell me in confidence what is the objective of this new offensive?' Hindenburg, a septuagenarian Titan who had been decorated for bravery in battle fifteen years before Mustafa was born, looked down magisterially at his presumptuous inter-locutor. Without a word, he offered Kemal a cigarette. The tobacco was Turkish.[10]

Kemal was unimpressed by what he was allowed to see of the German war machine. He found his hosts both arrogant and patronizing and, although he at first believed he was belatedly completing Vaheddin's education, it soon became clear to him that much of what was going on remained beyond the Prince's comprehension. The visit helped shape Kemal's conduct in the years ahead by confirming two of his prejudices: against the German alliance; and against the sultanate as an institution. As Vaheddin's brother, Sultan Mehmed V, was in his seventy-fourth year and in failing health, it was clear that the prince would soon inherit such lands as still remained within the Ottoman Empire. On earlier occasions in Ottoman history, an ambitious general would have considered three weeks in the company of the Sultan's heir a splendid opportunity for advancement in the coming reign. But Kemal saw no reason to ingra-tiate himself with so slight a 'Shadow of God on Earth.'

Sultan Mehmed V died on 2 July 1918 and Prince Vaheddin acceded as Mehmed VI. But Kemal was not in Constantinople when Enver escorted Turkey's new ruler, racked with rheumatism, to the mosque at Eyub for the ceremonial sword-girding, which corresponded to a coronation. Kemal's health had given way soon after the visit to Germany, and he was in great pain from a kidney complaint, complicated by the after-effects of a bout of gonorrhoea contracted long before but inadequately treated by unskilled physicians. Now he was sent to a hospital in Vienna for a month and then to the thermal springs at Carlsbad (later renamed Karlovy Vary), and it was in this Bohemian spa that he heard of Prince Vahideddin's accession.[11] Not until the end of July did he arrive back in the Turkish capital. He was received in audience by the new Sultan on three occasions, but no appointment was offered to him. Eventually he was informed by Enver that the Sultan would see him privately at Yildiz after Friday prayers. There he was ordered to return to Syria and take over the Seventh Army once more. As this posting came in the form of a personal command from the Sultan, Kemal could not refuse it. After nearly ten months of inaction at the peak period in the great conflict, Kemal set out again from Haydarpasa Station for Aleppo and Damascus. By now it was the second week of August 1918, and at German GHQ the apparently imperturbable Hindenburg and Ludendorff were beginning to question the ability of Germany and her allies to stave off defeat.

Kemal would have preferred to have been given command of all the Turkish forces in Palestine and Syria. But the Germans still sought to remain military overlords in the Levant. At least Kemal no longer had to contend with Falkenhayn; he had been transferred to the borderlands of Poland in March 1918 to keep watch on the Bolsheviks. Falkenhayn's successor in Palestine was Liman von Sanders, who knew the strength and failings of the Turkish soldiery better than any other German. On paper, Liman commanded 32,000 infantry with about 400 field guns and the specialists of the German Asia Corps which remained a formidable fighting force. His Turkish troops constituted three armies: the Eighth Army, on the coast south of Haifa; the Seventh, Kemal's command, stationed west of the Jordan, with headquarters at Nablus; and the Fourth, to the east of the Jordan. The whole army group was short of cavalry and lacked air support. Opposing them was an allied army of some 57,000 regular troops, with British, Australian and Indian contingents, supported by the Arab forces of the Emir Feisal and Colonel T.E. Lawrence, and by a French marine task force eager to seize Beirut. The commander-in-chief, General Allenby, had 12,000 cavalry horses which he intended to deploy imaginatively; he had shown skill in deceiving the enemy by feint concentration of troops and by planting fake plans of operations; and, although a traditional cavalryman himself, he understood the tactical use of aircraft. Liman and Kemal were faced by a far more formidable enemy than at Gallipoli.[12]

To Kemal's satisfaction he had serving under him as divisional commanders Ismet and Ali Fuad, his classmate at the Harbiye War College. So demoralized were the foot-soldiers that he needed good officers whom he could trust to hold them together. From reports reaching Nablus soon after Kemal's arrival it was clear that Allenby was contemplating an offensive in mid-September. But where would Allenby strike? All the evidence suggested a build-up around Jericho, immediately facing Kemal. An Indian Muslim deserter, brought to Nablus on Tuesday, 17 September, insisted that the offensive would begin on Thursday morning, with the main weight of the attack falling on the Turkish Eighth Army, near the coast, rather than up the Jordan. This information ran counter to all the intelligence reports. Was it simply another piece of deception?

Kemal's judgement had been right on Gallipoli; now, despite being confined to bed with a recurrence of his illness, he sifted the evidence and decided to accept the deserter's story. Liman, on the other hand, did not. When, on the Wednesday night, the first artillery bombardment opened up on Kemal's sector it seemed as if the Turk's intuition had let him down. Next morning, however, without any preliminary shelling, the British and Indian cavalry swept forward in the coastal sector with such impetus that the resistance of the Eighth Army was soon brushed aside. As the cavalry threatened to wheel to the right and envelop Nablus, Kemal hastily gave orders for a retreat across the River Jordan in the general direction of Damascus. So rapid was the Turkish collapse that, on the Thursday night, British cavalry almost captured Liman von Sanders in bed at his head-quarters in Nazareth.

Over the following six weeks Kemal preserved his claim never to have suffered defeat on the battlefield. But he was able to do so only through a series of brilliantly executed withdrawals. He ordered weary troops, short of food and supplies, back from Damascus to Rayak and on to Baalbek. Around him the deep hostility shown by the Arab peoples towards the Turks, who had so long been their masters, intensified Kemal's conviction that a sense of national identity counted for more than any shared Islamic faith. At his last meetings with Liman von Sanders and the German staff officers Kemal emphasized his intention of appealing to the Turkish national pride of his troops now that they were falling back on the natural geographical border of their homeland. Liman's last effec-tive order of the day handed over responsibility for protecting the approaches to Anatolia to Kemal, who was to concentrate what remained of the three Turkish armies in a single army group around Aleppo. But Liman's main concern was to bring back to Constan-tinople all the German and Austro-Hungarian officials and advisers clamouring for repatriation now that the Ottoman Empire was falling apart.

On 8 October Enver resigned as war minister and Talaat as Grand Vizier, advising Sultan Mehmed VI to appoint a government capable of reaching terms with the Entente allies. It was the end of the Young Turks trium-virate, its three leaders fleeing the country under German protection.[13] The new Grand Vizier was Izzet Pasha, who had worked amicably with Kemal in Kurdistan before becoming the Sultan's personal military adviser soon after his accession. Izzet appointed Hussein Rauf as Minister of Marine and summoned back Ismet to serve as Deputy War Minister. Kemal was convinced that he would soon receive instructions to report to Constantinople as Minister of War. But Izzet preferred to assume responsibility for the army himself; he did not want so strong and powerful a personality in the capital at a time when he was seeking peace terms. It was better for Kemal to construct defences above Aleppo, seek medical treatment to relieve the pain in his kidneys, and send fiery telegrams to Constantinople.

The Sultan agreed that the even-tempered Hussein Rauf should head an armistice delegation; and on 26 October the bearded Minister of Marine, together with an official from the foreign ministry and a colonel from the General Staff, arrived on the Greek island of Lemnos for talks aboard HMS *Agamemnon*, flagship of the British Mediterranean fleet. Conversations continued intermittently for five days until, on 30 October, an armistice was signed, as the battleship lay moored off Mudros: all Ottoman territories in Syria, Palestine, Mesopotamia and Arabia were to be placed under allied military government pending a peace treaty; the Dardanelles was to be cleared of mines; the forts of the Dardanelles and Bosphorus were to be occupied by allied troops; the Turkish army would demobilize, apart from units required to maintain internal order.

News of the Mudros armistice terms shocked Kemal.[14] He thought the terms so ill-defined that Rauf had connived at an unconditional surrender. Where, he demanded, was the boundary of Syria? The British, he complained, seemed to assume that it included the port of Alexandretta (later renamed Iskenderun) which had never been within the Ottoman province of Syria. Should he continue to defend the port, denying British, French and Indian troops access to the quays? If not, would Alexandretta be placed permanently outside Turkish sovereignty? Patiently Izzet and Rauf sent conciliatory replies, seeking to calm Kemal, but they failed to allay his fears. At last, eight days after the armistice was signed, he was told that his army group had ceased to exist. He should return at once to Constantinople.

On this occasion the train journey northwards took far longer. Not until 13 November did he step down once more at Haydarpasa Station. It was a black day for the homecoming of a proud military commander, still convinced that he was undefeated in the field. As he emerged from the station and looked across the waters towards Stamboul and Galata, a bitter spectacle greeted him; his return coincided with the arrival of the first British warships to sail up the mine-swept channel of the Dardanelles. Behind this vanguard could be seen vessels from all the allied navies, stretching back for sixteen miles into the Sea of Marmora. By dusk on that Wednesday the largest fleet ever to enter the Bosphorus rode at anchor off the Golden Horn, a visible proof to the Sultan and his subjects that the fate of the Ottoman Empire lay in the hands of its enemies.

War of Independence 3

When Rauf and his two companions set out for Mudros in October 1918 the Turks assumed they were seeking a peace settlement based upon 'Wilsonian principles'. So, indeed, did other armistice delegations despatched that autumn by the governments of Bulgaria, Austria, Hungary and Germany. Woodrow Wilson, the university professor who in 1912 became the first Democrat elected President of the United States in the twentieth century, was already widely respected as a visionary prophet; he offered an open diplomacy based upon nobler ideals than the discredited system of a balance of power. In January 1918 his famous address to Congress had laid down 'a programme of the world's peace': the twelfth of his 'Fourteen Points' stipulated that 'the Turkish portions of the present Ottoman Empire should be assured a secure sovereignty, but the other nationalities which are now under Turkish rule should be assured an undoubted security of life and an absolutely unmolested opportunity of autonomous development'; and he also proposed to open the Dardanelles for the free passage of ships from all nations under international guarantee.

Within a month of Wilson's speech to Congress, the

Turkish foreign minister accepted the principle that the nationalities within the Ottoman Empire should be granted institutions of their own. A 'Turkish Wilsonian League' of liberal intellectuals was set up in the Sultan's capital; it even proposed, during the first confused months of peace, that the United States should establish a protectorate over Turkey, to last for at least fifteen years. As the war ended, doubts remained over what future the liberator saviour in Washington would propose for Constantinople itself, where the Greek community was large and influential; but the Turks were confident that Wilson would rather safeguard the integrity of Turkey in Europe and Anatolia than accept the partition of the Ottoman Empire into spheres of influence. Even so hard-headed a realist as Kemal believed that Wilson would save Turkey from the crippling terms of a vindictive peace.

The Turks knew that the Entente allies – Britain, France, Tsarist Russia, Italy, Greece – had made a series of secret treaties which, by proposing partition, ran counter to Wilson's principles. Some commitments were by now invalid, for Lenin had repudiated all treaties made by Tsarist governments. But the Bolsheviks also published details of treaties found in the Petrograd archives: these showed, not merely that the allies had been contemplating the incorporation of Constantinople and the Straits within the Russian Empire, but that they had promised Italy the Turkish province of Adalia in Asia Minor, while France was to have a free hand in Syria, Lebanon and Cilicia and Great Britain in Palestine, the Jordan valley, Arabia and southern Mesopotamia. At the same time it was rightly suspected that the British and French had encouraged the Greek Prime Minister, Venizelos, to enter the war by promises of expansion in Asia Minor. Against all this dubious bargaining, the Turks clung to one hope. The United States had never been at war with the Ottoman Empire (or with Bulgaria). When the peace conference opened in Paris in January 1919 it was therefore felt that, since America had no specific objectives to attain in Thrace or Asia Minor, Turkey could count on President Wilson as a just arbitrator.

Too much faith was placed in the president's power and influence. The significance of mid-term elections which returned isolationist Republicans to the Congress was lost on people who were unfamiliar with the intricacies of the American political system; nor was sufficient allowance made for the voting strength of compact Greek communities in several predominantly Democrat states. No Turk had anticipated the effect of the immense charm and self-assurance of Venizelos on both Lloyd George (Britain's Prime Minister) and the American President during the early months of the Paris peace conference. 'Every time Venizelos sees Wilson the map of Europe is changed again,' a Yugoslav delegate to the peace conference was heard to complain.[1]

Preparation of the frontiers of the new Turkey was left to the work of expert committees – British, French, American. It was generally accepted that ethnically non-Turkish areas of the Ottoman Empire should be temporarily ceded to the allied powers as 'mandates', under the ultimate responsibility of the new League of Nations, to whom an annual report would be submitted by the mandatory authority. Thus Iraq, Palestine and Transjordan were placed under British mandate; and Syria and Lebanon under a French mandate. Yet, while the German treaty was signed at Versailles twenty-two weeks after the peace conference opened, there was never any hurry to settle the Eastern Question. Not until 17 June 1919 was a Turkish delegation received by the conference's principal executive body, the Council of Ten; and Wilson, who four weeks previously had agreed to seek Congressional approval for American mandates over Constantinople and Armenia, left for Washington twelve days later. There he was to find American opinion set hard against any lasting commitments in Europe or Asia; and he was therefore never able to play the role for which liberal Turks had cast him at the time of the Mudros armistice. Another year passed before, on 11 May 1920, the Sultan's government in Constantinople received the final settlement agreed in Paris. By then dramatic events were outpacing the peacemakers. Had the Great Powers moved swiftly and dictated a treaty while the Ottoman Empire was still shell-shocked by defeat, almost any terms would have been accepted without resistance; and, in that case, Kemal might well have followed the Young Turks triumvirate into obscurity. The long delay in preparing a settlement gave time for the growth of a sense of national identity among the proudly resilient Turks, whose new leaders ably exploited the conflicts of rival interests among the allied powers.

For six months after his return to Constantinople Mustafa Kemal remained a general without an army.[2] He leased a mansion at 25, Halaskargazi Avenue – now preserved as the 'Atatürk Museum', even though he only lived in it for a short time. The house, close to the Harbiye Barracks, formed a convenient meeting place for serving soldiers and active politicians who, like Kemal himself, were puzzled by the intentions of Sultan Mehmed VI. Turks received in audience by the Sultan were left in no doubt that he resented the allied presence: 'I can't look out of the window. I hate to see them,' he is reported to have said, nodding towards the warships in the Bosphorus. But he dissolved parliament at a time when the state of the Empire made it impossible to elect new deputies, and he appointed ministers who readily ingratiated themselves with the allied authorities. Kemal, who was granted an audience shortly after the dissolution of parliament, was confirmed in his conviction that the Sultan was a weak character. Yet it was becoming clear that he also possessed some of the wiliness of his half-brother, Abdul Hamid. During the uncertainties of that first winter of peace it seemed as if Mehmed VI was giving his political opponents a generous length of rope with which to hang themselves. Kemal, in particular, was allowed considerable freedom of activity, meeting old companions in arms so openly that there could be little doubt that he was encouraging the nucleus of a resistance movement.

The most bitter of all divisions in Constantinople and around the coast of Anatolia was the conflict between Turks and Greeks, an animosity based upon differences of race, religion and culture, and fed by folk memories which reached back to the dying years of Byzantium. During the early spring of 1919 rumours of the alleged concessions being made to Venizelos at the peace conference led to violent attacks by groups of Turks on isolated Greek communities, frequently provoking reprisals. Around Smyrna (now known as Izmir) a British naval presence sought to protect the Greeks, but along the Black Sea coast the responsibility for maintaining civil order rested with the Sultan's officials, many of whom were neither zealous nor efficient. So grave was the situation in the more remote districts that in April 1919 the British threatened the Sultan with total occupation of his country unless the anarchy was curbed. By devious expedients, remarkable even at the Sultan's court, Kemal's name was put forward as the Inspector-General best qualified to restore order along the Black Sea coast. His appointment – with a large staff of hand-picked senior officers and with powers making him virtually a pro-consul – was approved by the Sultan, who assured the British High Commissioner that he had 'complete confidence' in Mustafa Kemal Pasha's mission. In a farewell audience at Yildiz, Mehmed VI remarked cryptically to Kemal: 'Pasha, you can save the country'; and he presented him with a gold watch, on which was engraved the imperial arms.[3] With some hesitancy, the British put their stamp of approval on Kemal's visa. On the evening of 16 May Kemal boarded the *Bandirma*, a barely sea-worthy British-built coaster, and set out for the port of Samsun, an extremely rough voyage of some 400 miles along the Black Sea coast. He landed at Samsun sixty hours later, an event which Kemal decided was so important in his life that he later designated 19 May as his official birthday. It remains a holiday in the Turkish national calendar, although now devoted to youth and sport.

This third week in May 1919 was a time of great national emotion in Turkey. On the day before the *Bandirma* left Constantinople, a Greek army landed at Smyrna, covered by British, French and American warships. Local fanaticism exploded in casual shooting and in atrocious crimes committed against the Turks. The British admiral protested, while in Paris Venizelos deplored the violence; inevitably, the reports from Smyrna fanned the deep hatred of Turk for Greek in other parts of the Sultan's shrinking realm. Any leader who called on the Turks to defend their independence against foreign incursion at such at time could be certain of warm support in Anatolia. Yet Kemal moved circum-spectly: there was a small British army unit in Samsun with a commander who was highly suspicious of so formidable an Inspector-General.[4] After a week he left the coast for the interior, allegedly to ensure that the Havza district, where there had been guerrilla warfare between Greeks and Turks, was adequately policed.

His policing duties took a strange form, for it was at Havza that Kemal made the first of many stirring patriotic speeches, appealing to the pride of the Anatolian peasant warriors. However, when he heard that a British patrol was only a few miles north of the town, he went further up into the Anatolian plateau. Eventually he reached the old Hittite settlement of Amasya, ninety miles from the coast. With its wooden houses grouped around a fortress overhanging the gorge of the River Yesilirmak, the town was a natural base for a resistance movement. He was still 200 miles from Angora (now known as Ankara), at the centre of Anatolia, but communication along river valleys across the plateau was not difficult, and from Angora Kemal was joined by Rauf and Ali Fuad, both of whom he had talked with at length in Constantinople shortly before his departure. He knew, too, that he could rely on the support of General Kiazim Karabekir, commanding an army corps at Erzurum. From Amasya, on 21 June, Kemal issued a Declaration of Independence, calling on the Turkish people to send delegates to a national congress; Kemal insisted that it would meet in Anatolia since Mehmed VI, his capital and his administration were all under foreign duress. Two days later the Inspector-General was ordered to return to Constantinople. It was the first of many such summonses and threats. Not surprisingly, he defied the Sultan on each occasion. Eventually, on 8 July, Kemal resigned his commission.

The Turkish national movement gathered astonishing momentum between May and November 1919. But it was at first by no means certain that Kemal personally would set the pace. Much of his support came from former CUP members and from Muslim religious fanatics, towards whose basic political tenets he felt little sympathy. Moreover, in eastern Turkey the initiative had been taken by Kiazim Karabekir who had at his command a powerful nucleus for an army of defiance. But 'Mustafa Kemal of Anafarta' enjoyed greater prestige than any other Turkish soldier, as both Kiazim and Ali Fuad recognized. Largely through the diplomatic skill of Rauf, he was accepted as chairman of a congress at Erzurum which had been conceived by Kiazim some weeks before the sailing of the *Bandirma*. Thereafter Kemal's leadership of the movement of national regeneration was never seriously in question.

The principal task of the Erzurum Congress was to

draft what become known as the National Pact, the basic manifesto of Kemalism during the struggle for independence. The Pact insisted on a right of self-determination for the ethnic Turks, the preservation and inviolability of the Turkish lands, the election of a provisional government, and the withdrawal of privileges granted to minorities living within the Turkish heartland. Copies of the manifesto were circulated widely in Turkey itself. Thanks to the initiative of Colonel Rawlinson, a British officer in Erzurum, the National Pact even reached London, where it impressed Lord Curzon, the Foreign Secretary; he confessed to fears that 'the weakest and most abject of our foes would end by achieving the greatest triumph.' In September, a second congress met at Sivas, convened in response to Kemal's Amasya declaration. Only thirty-nine delegates could make the journey to Sivas, far fewer than Kemal had hoped, but the congress strengthened his hand, as it endorsed the Erzurum programme of action.[5]

In 1909 the Young Turks had marched from Salonika on Constantinople and frustrated Abdul Hamid's counter-revolution. To have attempted a similar feat of arms from inner Anatolia ten years later would have ended in disaster. Allied forces held the forts of the Bosphorus and Dardanelles and controlled key strategic points along the basic trunk railways; a Greek army held Smyrna and its hinterland; the Italians were at Adalkia (now known as Antalya); the French at Alexandretta; the British in strength in Mesopotamia. Rather than risk war, Kemal and Rauf encouraged sympathizers in the capital to put pressure on the Sultan's government. In November elections were held for a new Turkish parliament to meet, as before, in Constantinople. Kemal's 'National Movement' won a substantial majority. It could now claim impeccable democratic legitimacy.

Kemal would not return to Constantinople; he feared a coup by his political enemies, backed by the British. Instead, he established himself in Angora, a town he had never visited before. Deputies travelled out there to consult him, for it was not until the third week in January 1920 that the parliamentary session began. There was a token occupation force in Angora: a British detachment at the railway station; and Tunisians keeping the French tricolor flying over what had been the club of the local CUP members. Kemal established close links with the French, who were soon secretly supplying him with surplus arms, and he had already made contact with the Italians. The British, however, remained hostile, both in Anatolia and at Constantinople. The parliamentary session proved short-lived, as Kemal had suspected. On 28 January the deputies duly ratified the National Pact, making it an approved statement of intent. The British were alarmed, fearing grave riots when the proposed terms of the peace treaty were known; and on 16 March British soldiers, sailors and marines formally occupied the capital, taking over the Turkish War Ministry and arresting more than eighty deputies suspected of fomenting unrest. Next day Sultan Mehmed VI received a delegation of deputies, including Rauf, at Yildiz. They urged him to remember that Anatolia was 'a ring of steel', free from intimidation by any army of occupation; and they begged him not to sign a treaty without the consent of parliament. Coldly and silently the Sultan broke off the audience.[6]

For Kemal the occupation of Constantinople formed a decisive break. He reacted with alacrity. Individual British commissioners and small detachments were rounded up and placed under arrest. Defiant proclamations were telegraphed to distant towns in Turkey and to the world press: the Sultan must now be regarded as a prisoner of the foreigner, unable to exercise freely his religious duties as Caliph; all Turkish patriots should hasten to Angora where, since parliament was intimidated in the capital, a 'Grand National Assembly' would meet in the fourth week of April 'with extraordinary powers'. The

Sultan respónded by denouncing the Nationalists as rebels. With Allied support, he raised an army which he concentrated at Izmit, a small port at the head of the Sea of Marmara commanding rail and road routes from the Bosphorus into Anatolia. At the same time, irregular troops – virtually bandits – were encouraged to attack towns and villages which gave support to Kemal. The Nationalists also had irregulars of their own, Zeybeks from the mountains behind Smyrna, who were led by a close friend of Kemal, Colonel Refet, one of the 'founding fathers' who sailed with him to Samsun. All Anatolia was ravaged by a bitter civil war that spring.

Had Kemal been a War Lord leading an insurrection he would have concentrated on military matters – and would soon have lost his following. Instead, he gambled on the future. Ankara (as the Nationalists called Angora) became an embryonic capital. The CUP Club, evacuated by Tunisian troops, served as the home of the Grand National Assembly, with 115 deputies packed into a chamber resembling a large village school-room. An Ankara carpenter presented a rostrum for the Speaker, varnished desks were brought from the teachers' training college, two oil lamps and iron stoves came from local coffee-houses. There were smaller halls for a Council of Ministers and committees, a 'Speaker's Office', used by Kemal and, next to it, a small room where the faithful could answer the calls to prayer; for, despite Kemal's natural secularism, he had no wish at this time to offend Muslim susceptibilities. Tobacco and alcohol were strictly forbidden, although there was a café not far away for those who wished to indulge in such vices. Most members of the assembly found accommodation in the dormitories of a teacher's training college, to which Kemal would come occasionally, sitting on a bed and explaining his political objectives to deputies confused by the threat of change in a society which had remained static for so long. It was strange enough for them to find a woman, Halide Edib, among Kemal's six closest political associates. Another fifteen years were to pass before Turkish women could enjoy the full rights of citizenship.[7]

Kemal moved cautiously. There were no revolutionary decrees, as in Soviet Russia, for he accepted the fundamentally conservative temperament of the deputies and their instinctive desire for continuity in government. The provisional constitution adopted in January 1921 emphasized the 'sovereignty of the people', but retained the monarchical concept of a Sultan, although he would not exercise authority until liberated from 'pressure and coercion'. The deputies agreed to more innovations than they realized: executive power was entrusted to the Council of Ministers, a cabinet of nine men chosen by Kemal, although requiring the approval of the deputies. This first Grand National Assembly met regularly until April 1923: often it was critical of Kemal's day-to-day policies; occasionally it was obstreperous; but as a safety-valve for an explosive people who mistrusted westernization it proved invaluable.

Early in June 1920 the allied peace terms became known in Turkey. They caused consternation.[8] The loss of the Arab lands of the Ottoman Empire had been expected, but it was now proposed to place the Dardanelles and the Bosphorus under international control, to limit the Turkish army to a token defence force, to put Turkey's finances and national gendarmerie under foreign control, to establish an autonomous Kurdistan and an independent Armenia with access to the Black Sea, and to cede to Greece all eastern Thrace, up to within twenty miles of Constantinople, and eight islands in the Aegean. Moreover the Greeks were to occupy and administer Smyrna and its hinterland for five years, after which a plebiscite should determine whether the territory was to come under Greek sovereignty or remain Turkish. These terms were duly accepted by the Sultan, whose plenipotentiaries signed the treaty embodying them on 10 August at Sèvres – the Paris suburb where, as the wits pointed out, fragile porcelain was manufactured.

In April Marshal Foch had told the allies that they would require an army of twenty-seven divisions if they intended to enforce such terms on Turkey, but his advice was ignored. Even before the treaty was signed, a wave of indignation rallied support behind Kemal. The peace terms transformed a civil war into a war of independence. So demoralized was the Sultan's army on the Izmit peninsula that it virtually disintegrated, allowing Kemal's forces to reach the Sea of Marmara, where they were halted by shellfire from the allied warships. At this point Venizelos offered to assist the allies; in return for financial backing, the well-equipped Greek army would go forward, clear Thrace of any incipient Kemalist pockets of resistance, and sweep the Nationalists out of western Anatolia, thereby relieving all pressure on Constantinople. The French were unenthusiastic and the Italians hostile, but Lloyd George – who greatly admired Venizelos – gave the project his full support.

The Greeks launched their assault on 22 June. Within two and a half weeks they accomplished all that Venizelos had promised, even capturing historic Brusa (renamed Bursa), the Ottoman capital for almost a century before the fall of Byzantium and still the fourth largest town in Turkey. Kemal advocated an orderly withdrawal in depth: the Turks would retire to the heights of the Anatolian plateau, tempting the Greeks to move deeper and deeper into the interior, their thin columns thrusting eastwards and away from their coastal bases. Kemal held good to this strategy for two years before mounting a decisive counter-offensive; it was similar to Marshal Kutuzov's masterplan of 1812 which used the vastness of Russia to draw Napoleon away from his supply depots until the ravages of winter brought disaster to his army.

The Turkish Nationalists received support from an

unexpected quarter. For the Sèvres settlement caused anger in Moscow as well as in Ankara. The new Soviet government was appalled at the prospect of foreign warships moving freely into the Black Sea, with no Russian representative on the international commission controlling the Straits. Nor could the Bolsheviks accept an American-sponsored independent Armenia. From May 1920 onwards there was increasingly close collaboration between Moscow and Ankara, despite Turkey's lack of interest in ideological Marxism. Briefly Kemal even corresponded with Enver, who had found sanctuary in Moscow, still hoping to create a unified Islamic state in central Asia which would have a special relationship both with the Bolsheviks and with the effective government of Turkey. Kemal wanted arms and money from Russia and collaboration against Armenian nationalism. At the same time, he recognized General Kiazim's desire to turn eastwards from Erzurum and recover lands annexed by Tsar Alexander II forty years before. Disappointment with Soviet offers, and with a grandiose 'Congress of Peoples of the East' which met in Soviet Baku early in September, made Kemal sanction Kiazim's advance into Armenia at the end of the month. By early November 1920 Kars was in Turkish hands and General Ail Fuad, who had failed to hold Bursa against the Greeks, was sent to Moscow as Kemal's first ambassador where, soon after his arrival, he negotiated with Stalin a treaty defining the frontiers in the Caucasus, which has survived until the present day. At the same time the Turks began to receive surplus weapons and munitions from the Russians with which to carry on the fight against Western imperialism. The most tragic sufferers from these events were the Armenians, as so often had been the case over the previous quarter of a century. Although the Armenian state, proposed in the Treaty of Sèvres, existed only on paper, the mere threat of its creation intensified the ruthless hostility of Turks and Russians towards every aspect of Armenian life and culture.

While the agreements in Moscow effectively locked the back door to the Anatolian homeland, the principal threat remained in the West. Yet, as the Greek army was poised to march into Anatolia in the autumn of 1920, a strange shift in domestic politics suddenly threw into doubt the future of the whole campaign. The young King Alexander of the Hellenes was bitten by a pet monkey on 27 September; his wound turned septic and he died four weeks later. This tragedy at once threw Greece into constitutional crisis: a majority of the people wished for the return to the throne of Alexander's father, Constantine I, who had been exiled in 1917 under pressure from the French and British for allegedly being 'pro-German'. A general election followed Alexander's death in mid-November, with royalist sentiment swinging against Venizelos and forcing him out of office and into exile. Early in December Greek voters went again to the polls and in a plebiscite decided overwhelmingly in favour of King Constantine's return to the throne. He was back in Athens before Christmas.

Constantine's restoration had immediate political consequences in Anatolia. Although the French and British had encouraged Venizelos to build up a considerable Greek military presence in Asia Minor, they were not prepared to give similar military and financial aid to a king whom they held in deep mistrust. A representative of Kemal's government in Ankara was even invited to an inter-allied conference in London in February and March 1921, where he made little impression on Lloyd George but reached working agreements with both the French premier and the Italian Foreign Minister. It would therefore have been judicious in those early months of 1921 for King Constantine to seek terms from Kemal and withdraw from Asia Minor. But Constantine, whose army had captured Salonika during the Balkan Wars, did not wish to begin his second reign by surrendering the gains promised to Greece by the Treaty of Sèvres. He believed

that if the better-equipped Greek army could win a major
battle against the Turkish Nationalist forces, he would
recover from London and Paris complete support for the
fulfilment of the peace settlement. Although the super-
session of Venizelists by royalist officers led to
uncertainty in the army command, the King and his
General Staff were confident of gaining at least one significant victory.

Ever since the fall of Bursa, Kemal had anticipated a
major Greek offensive which would threaten Ankara and
the fragile structure of his embyronic 'new Turkey'.[9] A
ministry of defence was set up in Ankara, headed by
General Fevzi, who was the Sultan's War Minister when
Kemal went to Samsun but who defected in April 1920.
Fevzi and Kemal assigned the southern sector of the
Front to Colonel Refet and the north-western sector to
Colonel Ismet, who deployed some 23,000 men in strong
defensive positions. The first assault came in January
1921, before the conference opened in London. Four
Greek infantry divisions, based on Bursa, thrust south-
eastwards towards the town of Eskişehir, a key railway
junction where the line from the Haydarpasa Station on
the Bosphorus divides, one branch going to Ankara (135
miles to the east) and the other continuing southwards
towards Konya and Adana. The Greeks were checked to
the west of Eskişehir by Ismet, whose headquarters were
in the small town of Inönü, a few miles south of the railway and commanding the last ridge before the plain in
which Eskişehir stands. It was a harsh terrain: a succession of mountainous ridges, broken by a few valleys. Yet
it was not unlike the southern fringe of the Balkan chain
in Macedonia, where Greeks and Turks were old contes-
tants. On this occasion, however, the offensive began in
the second week of January and the weather was bitterly
cold. Snow and ice covered the higher ground while mud
hampered the movement of horses, field guns and
mechanized transport down in the valleys. The Greeks

made little progress. Yet, to their amazement, Ismet mounted a sustained counter-attack, throwing them back through the mud and slush, with snow sweeping down as they tried to extricate guns and wagons. So spirited a resistance convinced the Greeks they would not break through until the coming of spring. They retired in good order to Bursa.

Their offensive was resumed on 23 March. On this occasion a larger Greek army group advanced from Smyrna on a more southerly railway junction at the town of Afyonkarahisar, which the Turks could not hold. To Kemal's relief, this Greek force then turned southwards towards Konya rather than march northwards on Eskişehir, which was again under attack from the northern army group. The fighting for Inönü continued for a whole week. After suffering heavy casualties, and with all their resources fully committed to the battle, the Greeks at last broke through and were poised to debouch into the plain. But, to their consternation, they came under intensive and accurate artillery fire which checked them until Ismet brought up cavalry reserves, driving the exhausted Greek troops back off the escarpment they had seized at such heavy cost of life. By the beginning of April all was quiet again on the Anatolian Front. Kemal made certain that the Grand National Assembly celebrated the second battle of Inönü as an important victory. Morale was high in Ankara that spring.

A few weeks later, early in June 1921, King Constantine landed at Smyrna, prepared to lead the Greek armies to victory. He was a gifted strategist and the Turks interpreted his coming as evidence that a major thrust towards Ankara was imminent. The King spoke confidently to western journalists; none realized that he was gravely ill, with only two and a half years to live. Not since Napoleon III set out from Paris in 1870 at the start of the Franco-Prussian War had so desperately sick a sovereign assumed supreme command of armies in the field. Constantine remained in Anatolia for three months; he was never able to exercise active leadership, although he helped prepare the general plan of operations, making certain that his senior officers avoided the strategic error they had made in the spring. In this third offensive along the trunk railway the Greek army was concentrated in three main columns: one struck south-eastwards from Bursa again; a second headed for the small railhead town of Kutahya, further south; but the main assault was on the Afyonkarahisar sector, and this time General Papoulas, the Greek chief-of-staff, turned northwards so as to threaten the railway link between Eskişehir and Ankara rather than pressing towards Konya. It seemed probable that Ismet's defences would be outflanked. Kemal hurried from Ankara to Ismet's field headquarters and ordered him, with great reluctance, to abandon Eskişehir and fall back eastwards along the railway, thus drawing the Greeks deeper into Anatolia. A new defensive line was prepared along the Sakarya River, in places barely fifty miles from Ankara.

On either side of the Sakarya there is a bare dun-coloured plain, with rough grass and stubble near the river. In summer it is a low stream cutting its way in a succession of small gorges across a terrain which, without the Sakarya and its tributaries, would have crumbled into desert. Further back from the river are some low hills and a long ridge, the Chal Dag, with a broad and flat hump which commanded the railway and gave a clear view across the plain as far as the site of Gordium, the capital of ancient Phyrgia, which stood on the right bank of the river. Chal Dag was not a good defensive position: its slopes were open, with little scrub, and the rock-face was so hard that it was almost impossible to dig trenches. But the Sakarya and its tributaries offered Kemal the best chance of halting the Greek advance. The absence of water-holes in the arid districts to north and south made it unlikely that the Greeks would seek to outflank the Turkish line.

In the second week of August 1921 Kemal decided to take command of the army on the Sakarya himself, with Fevzi as Chief of the General Staff. He arrived at Polatli railway station immediately west of Chal Dag, on 12 August, with a Greek attack imminent. At once he rode up one of the foothills and studied the distant lines of dust which showed the movement of Greek transport. But as Kemal lit a cigarette, his horse took fright and threw him so violently on the ground that he broke a rib. For the next three weeks he commanded the army, not from the saddle but from a seat, brought from a railway carriage, in a mud-walled cottage on high ground, equidistant from Ankara and the river itself. Tactical decisions he left to Fevzi, for his injuries kept him away from the front line. Yet somehow, as at Gallipoli six years before, he cajoled and inspired the Turkish soldiery into offering a fanatical resistance. Undernourished peasants, many of them living skeletons in tattered uniforms, steeled themselves to defend desperately a swathe of featureless plateau, some sixty miles wide and twelve miles deep.

The battle of the Sakarya raged for twenty-two days, with heavy casualties on both sides. The Greek infantry suffered in particular from Turkish cavalry, on wild and emaciated horses who disputed possession of hard-won gains. The fiercest fighting was on the Chal Dag ridge, which fell to the Greeks after four days of sustained assault; but the Turks were able to summon reserves westwards from Erzurum and Sivas while the Greeks were too far from their base at Smyrna and too dependent on shipping to keep their expeditionary force in being. When the fighting died away along the Sakarya on 13 September, both sides claimed victory. The Greeks had not taken Ankara and they were forced to fall back west of the river; but they still held the key positions along the railways of Anatolia, giving them control of a huge area in Asia Minor. The Turks, on the other hand, had blunted the great offensive; they doubted if the Greeks would ever again be able to launch so formidable an attack in the depths of Anatolia. After Sakarya, the Grand National Assembly honoured Kemal with the rank of Marshal of the Army and the traditional title of Ghazi, 'victor against the infidel'. Of more immediate practical significance was the French government's despatch to Ankara of a senior diplomat who, on 20 October, signed a separate treaty with the Turks. The French, always logical realists in their statecraft, had thus decided that the Kemalist régime merited diplomatic recognition; if the terms of the Treaty of Sèvres were unattainable, better tear it up as swiftly as possible. France abandoned attempts to build up a privileged position in Cilicia in return for the promise of commercial concessions once peace was fully restored. At the same time the French supplied Kemal with considerable quantities of arms and munitions.

There were repeated attempts in that winter of 1921–22 to halt the fighting and negotiate a peaceful settlement in Asia Minor. Foreign ministers conferred in London, Paris, Rome and Venice. Fethi, who served as Kemal's Minister of the Interior, travelled to the western European capitals and was well received by the French but cold-shouldered by the British Foreign Secretary, Curzon. In Ankara many members of the Grand National Assembly, including some of Kemal's close colleagues, would have accepted a compromise, but the Ghazi was adamant. He insisted that the Greeks must evacuate Anatolia before an armistice was signed. For the moment he was prepared to wait; Turkey grew militarily stronger month by month, while it was clear that political disputes were eroding the cohesion of the Greek armies.

In the last days of July 1922 the Greeks made an extraordinary move. To improve his country's inter-

national standing General Hadjianestis, the newly
appointed Greek commander-in-chief, withdrew two
divisions from central Anatolia, shipped them to Thrace
and threatened to enter Constantinople, which was
lightly held by British, French and Italian units. Briefly
there was a risk of conflict between the Greeks and the
inter-allied army of occupation; British and French troops
manned the Chatalja defences to the west of Constantinople, and a powerful march force was concentrated in the
Sea of Marmara. But the Greeks never marched into
Constantinople. For Hadjianestis's action convinced Kemal
that the moment had come for a Turkish offensive in
Anatolia. In withdrawing two divisions from Asia to Europe,
the Greeks had tipped the military balance in his favour.
Throughout August Greek intelligence reports noted
clouds of dust arising day after day from the roads
between Ankara and the Sakarya, with a long line of
camp-fires in the evening sky suggesting a massive
Turkish concentration of troops in the hills beside the
railway. Around Eskişehir and İnönü the Greeks were on
the alert for another clash of arms over a familiar battlefield.

Kemal, as commander-in-chief, was on a hilltop in the
front line at dawn on Saturday, 26 August, when the
Turkish offensive began. But that hill was nowhere near
Eskişehir; for the dust clouds and camp-fires were a ruse;
in the Sakarya sector a weakened Turkish army corps
stood on the defensive; the main Turkish army, brought
slowly to the battle-zone in a succession of overnight
marches, was concentrated more than eighty miles from
Eskişehir, in the mountains beyond Afyonkarahisar and
south of Dumlupinar. They were 200 miles inland from
Smyrna; but Kemal's order of the day was laconic and
precise: 'Armies, your primary objective is the Mediterranean. Forward.'[10]

General Hadjianestis's headquarters were at Smyrna,
aboard a ship; he soon lost touch with the battle as

Turkish cavalry swept forward and cut the telephone wires. The Greeks had fought valiantly in a succession of wars over the past ten years, but the surprise and vigour of the Turkish offensive overwhelmed them. Defeat on that first morning of battle became a rout when, later on that same day, the Turks overturned defences carefully constructed during the long lull of the preceding months. Within ten days the Turkish armies had split their adversaries into two, gaining as decisive a victory as the Germans were to achieve in France in 1940 by their thrust to the Channel coast. What remained of the Greek expeditionary force was evacuated from Smyrna on Friday, 8 September, leaving behind 50,000 prisoners of war.

Early next morning Turkish cavalry entered Smyrna and found British naval landing parties in the streets. Even though Kemal maintained that Great Britain and Turkey were still at war (since he did not recognize the Treaty of Sèvres) the Royal Marines remained on guard at the gasworks and other British-owned properties throughout the weekend. They were there when Kemal himself drove through the town on the Sunday morning, with an escort of lancers around his car, which was decorated with olive branches. Turkish regular troops remained well disciplined; irregular fighters and civilians with grievances against Greek and Armenian shopowners committed terrible atrocities, especially after Kemal left the port for his headquarters in the Karsyaka district. On Wednesday afternoon – 13 September – observers aboard British warships offshore saw several columns of smoke arising from the Armenian quarter of the city. A strong wind blew the flames through the most prosperous districts, forcing Kemal to evacuate his headquarters. 'What I see as I stand on the deck of the *Iron Duke* is an unbroken wall of fire, two miles long, in which twenty distinct volcanoes of raging flames are throwing up jagged, writhing tongues to a height of a hundred feet,' reported

George Ward Price, the *Daily Mail*'s ace war correspondent.[11] Many thousands of homes were destroyed in a fire which spared the Muslim quarter of the city but destroyed old, historic Christian Smyrna. As with the great fires of Moscow in 1812, Varna in 1854 and Salonika in 1917, nobody can identify the arsonists responsible for so terrible a tragedy. The pathetic Greek refugees who sought sanctuary aboard the foreign warships – nearly a quarter of a million men, women and children – all blamed the Turks. The Turkish authorities pointed out that Greeks had been firing towns and villages in a 'scorched earth' policy as they fell back across Anatolia and that it was not in Kemal's interest for three-quarters of the port to be left a gaunt, charred ruin.

There remained a final act in Turkey's dramatic struggle for independence from foreign rule. Kemal was prepared to carry the war into Europe in order to attain the frontiers claimed for Turkey in the National Pact. At least one hot-headed adviser urged him to reclaim western Thrace and march on his birthplace, Salonika, so as to wipe out the humiliations of the Balkan Wars. Kemal, however, limited himself to what he believed was attainable. Turkish troops moved hurriedly towards the Dardanelles, crossing a 'neutral zone' established by the Treaty of Sèvres, some fifty miles in depth and extending as far south as Edremit. Around Chanak itself a thin line of British troops held the 'Zone of the Straits', twelve miles deep; their commander, General Tim Harington, had orders to halt any Turkish penetration in this area.[12]

Ten days after the great fire at Smyrna, a squadron of British Hussars encountered Turkish infantry on the edge of the Zone of the Straits, close to the excavations at the site of Troy. The British retired behind barbed wire; the Turkish units arrived and dug themselves in, facing the British. No shots were fired; there was even some fraternization. But in London a war crisis loomed ominously and unexpectedly. Alarmist headlines appeared in the evening newspapers on 16 September and recurred frequently until the end of the month. Public opinion was set firmly against any new military adventures. There were a series of 'Stop the War' demonstrations in Britain, many of them backed by the more widely read Conservative newspapers. But Lloyd George – still Prime Minister of the coalition – and Churchill, his Colonial Secretary, believed that it was essential to 'keep the Turks out of Europe'. As early as 7 September the Prime Minister had told his cabinet: 'In no circumstances could we allow the Gallipoli Peninsula to be held by the Turks. It was the most important strategic position in the world.'[13] The British government sought backing from the French, Italians, Romanians and Serbs as well as from the Dominions, but apart from a token response in New Zealand, no other government was prepared to risk war in order to keep Kemal from the Straits.

Fortunately both General Harington and Sir Horace Rumbold, the British High Commissioner in Constantinople, showed good sense and moderation. Harington never delivered to the Turks an ultimatum drafted by the British cabinet because, as he telegraphed to London, he was sure it would 'put a match' to the crisis. Instead, the quiet diplomacy of Harington and Rumbold induced the Turks to accept an informal conference at Mudania to discuss the future of the Straits, the neutral zone and eastern Thrace. This triumph of common sense speedily brought the Chanak Crisis to an end; accidentally it also precipitated the fall of the coalition government, for Lloyd George's Conservative partners shared the widespread alarm at the apparent irresponsibility with which he so nearly drifted into war.

The conference at Mudania, the seaport for Bursa, opened on 1 October.[14] It was attended by Harington, representatives of Italy and France and by General Ismet as Kemal's spokesman. After ten days of talks the 'Mudania Convention' was signed: the Turks agreed to withdraw from the borders of the neutral zone and allow the allies to remain in occupation of Constantinople, Chanak and the Gallipoli peninsula until a peace treaty could be negotiated to replace the unacceptable Sèvres settlement. Before leaving Constantinople, Harington telegraphed to London to say that he expected to meet Kemal in person. The Ghazi, however, was not prepared to sit down at a conference table. Rather than go to Mudania, he chose to return to Ankara to address the Grand National Assembly. There, in the provincial centre which he was building into a capital city, he basked in a hero's welcome orchestrated by deputies who had begun to doubt his strategic reasoning so long as the Greeks were entrenched along Ankara's railroute to the West. Victory over Kemal's external enemies was now assured. There remained, of course, Sultan Mehmed VI, powerless in his palace at Yildiz. But for how long would the Ghazi allow a symbol of defunct authority to claim sovereignty over the Turkish State?

Revolution from Above 4

From his earliest days as a military cadet Mustafa Kemal had been receptive to Western ideas, like many intelligent youngsters born in Macedonia and Thrace. Most Turks, however, were natural conservatives who feared change as a forerunner of social upheaval. The Sultanate had evolved through nine centuries of history; its form was shaped by interpretations of the Sacred Law of the Prophet Mohammed, by traditions inherited from the Byzantine Court, and by the practical needs of a multi-national empire, accustomed to accept the 'Peoples of Scripture' – Christians and Jews – as vassal subjects of a Muslim sovereign. This political basis of government was enhanced in 1517 by a newly acquired spiritual authority when Sultan Selim I became Caliph, a title hitherto borne by rulers in Baghdad and Cairo. As sultans and caliphs, Selim's successors claimed the leadership of Islam throughout the world. If the victorious Turkish Nationalists wished to impose reforms on the sultanate in 1922, they would therefore encounter hostility not only from political traditionalists but, more ominously, from deeply religious upholders of the faith.

Kemal himself was inclined to sweep away the sultanate

and caliphate root and branch, counting on his personal popularity to frustrate opposition in the Grand National Assembly. But two of the founding fathers of the National Movement, Refet and Rauf, persuaded him to move cautiously. They thought that the Sultan could become a constitutional sovereign, the Muslim equivalent of the monarchs of Britain, the Netherlands and Scandinavia; he should retain the caliphate because it would serve as an instrument to give a modernized Turkey influence in other Islamic lands. Kemal compromised: he assured the deputies in the Assembly that the future of the sultanate was not in dispute; but he insisted that the Ankara government should have a representative at Constantinople. He therefore appointed the courageous cavalry officer Refet as military governor of western Thrace, with his headquarters in the Sultan's capital. In effect, he was Kemal's pro-consul.

When Refet landed at Saraybürnü, the entrance to the Golden Horn, on the afternoon of 22 October 1922, he received the Constantinople equivalent of a ticker-tape welcome: ships' sirens, festooned flags and bunting, a forest of portraits of the Ghazi held on poles above the onlookers' heads, the sacrifice of rams in the streets. But when the heir to the throne and two aides of the Sultan came to greet Refet they were coldly received. He recognized only ministers and officials appointed by the government in Ankara. Kemal telegraphed his approval of Refet's conduct.[1]

Ten days after Refet reached the Golden Horn, the British and French invited both the Sultan and the National Assembly in Ankara to send envoys to the international conference at Lausanne which would draw up a revised peace treaty. There was anger in the Grand National Assembly that the Sultan and his puppet 'ministers' should be placed on an equal footing with the 'Government of the Nation'. Kemal exploited this mood to propose the abolition of the sultanate, although not of the caliphate. A draft law, rushed through the Assembly, declared that when the British troops occupied the capital in March 1920 sovereignty had passed from the Sultan to the people. It also affirmed the right of the Turkish nation to decide who, 'in learning and character', was the most worthy person to hold the office of Caliph. Mehmed VI was given notice to quit, although as yet no coercion would be used against him.

The Sultan's puppet ministers surrendered their seals of office; the municipal administration of the capital acknowledged the authority of the military governor of Eastern Thrace; and, at the Yildiz Palace, Sultan Mehmed VI, fearing speedy assassination, put himself under the protection of General Harington's troops. Early in the morning of 11 November he was smuggled out of Yildiz in a British army ambulance. At his own request, the Sultan was given sanctuary aboard HMS *Malaya*, one of the battleships whose presence in the Bosphorus he had so deplored. The warship sailed as soon as he was aboard. Within a few days he was in Malta, finally settling at San Remo, where he died three and a half years later.[2]

As soon as news reached Ankara of the fallen Sultan's flight, Kemal instructed Refet to invite Mehmed VI's cousin, Abdul Mejid, to become Caliph. Abdul Mejid assumed the office of spiritual leader of Islam on 25 November in a ceremony carefully scrutinized by Refet to ensure that he received none of the honours due to a Sultan. For the moment Turkey was an empire without an emperor; sovereignty was vested with 'the people' through their deputies in the Grand National Assembly, although effective power was in the hands of the Council of Ministers, under Kemal's presidency. It was Kemal who decided that Rauf, an experienced diplomat, should serve as Prime Minister rather than go to Lausanne for the peace conference. That task he gave to Ismet who was now officially appointed foreign minister. Even though Ismet felt little inclination to accept the post, he regarded himself as a soldier of the state and automatically obeyed the Ghazi's command. Rauf, who had no opinion of Ismēt as a diplomat, would have preferred to head the deputation to Lausanne himself. Kemal, however, had faith in the tenacious defender of Eskişehir; Ismet was a methodical chief-of-staff, and had already shown some skill in negotiation at Mudania during the Chanak Crisis. But Rauf resented the apparently inconsequential manner in which Kemal would shuffle his cabinet, as if the ministers were of no greater consequence to him than playing cards. To Rauf, and to several other old colleagues, it seemed that the Ghazi was becoming increasingly reluctant to take advice.

The Lausanne Conference opened on 20 November.[3] Ismet, new to round-table diplomacy, found it hard to trim his Mudania style of negotiation so as to counter the wiles of such experienced veterans as Venizelos and Lord Curzon, the British Foreign Secretary. Among innovations at the peace conference was the presence of a delegation from Soviet Russia, headed by Georgy Chicherin, the Commissar for Foreign Affairs. It was not difficult for Curzon, as chairman, to convince Britain's wartime partners that Chicherin the Bolshevik and Ismet the Nationalist were in accord, thus increasing their suspicion of the Turks. Reports of the discussions reaching Ankara exasperated Rauf, who complained that Ismet was outmanoeuvred by the Western allies. As the conference dragged on into the New Year, the mood of the National Assembly hardened against the Foreign Minister; deputies blamed him for failing to secure within Turkey's frontiers the oil-rich northernmost province of Iraq, Mosul. Yet Ismet firmly resisted attempts to perpetuate the system of 'Capitulations', the privileges granted by successive Sultans to foreign financiers and entrepreneurs which exempted them from paying Turkish taxes or from prosecution in Turkish courts. He was, in a sense, fighting a diplomatic war of attrition, counting on mounting discord between the British and the French, but in Ankara the deputies failed to understand his tactics. When, in the first week of February 1923, an impatient Curzon broke up the conference with no formal agreement over the 'Capitulations', Ismet returned apprehensively to Ankara to face a series of stormy meetings of the Assembly.

Kemal consistently gave Ismet warm support at these sessions. By now, however, the Assembly had begun to resent their President's authoritarian ways. Among the dignitaries at Lausanne for the opening of the conference was Italy's Prime Minister, Benito Mussolini, whose 'march on Rome' had inaugurated the Fascist Era a few weeks before; but in that winter of 1922–23, the Ghazi seemed more openly dictatorial than Italy's new Duce. In December 1922 there was a clumsy parliamentary attempt to keep Kemal in check when a small group of deputies proposed a law by which membership of the government and election to the Assembly should be confined to people born within the 1922 boundaries of Turkey or resident within them for the past five years. Had this proposal been carried into law, it would have excluded Kemal, who was born in Salonika and whose military obligations had prevented him from living contin- uously inside Turkey for the required period. But most deputies realized that public support for Kemal was still so strong that ordinances of this kind merely served to make them look ridiculous.

More threatening to Kemal's position was the Ali Shükru affair, in February 1923.[4] There had long been deep mistrust between the Ghazi and the deputy for Trabzon, Ali Shükru, who was a devout Muslim fanatic. During one of the Grand National Assembly's debates on the slow progress of negotiations at Lausanne, Ali Shükru suddenly delivered a personal attack on Kemal, criticizing him for following an impious way of life and, in particular, for drinking alcohol heavily. When Fethi – Kemal's old friend, now minister of the interior – counter-attacked with accusations of misappropriated funds, Ali Shükru's denunciation of the Ghazi became even more extravagant: Kemal was planning to have himself proclaimed Sultan, he declared. On the day after this wild outburst in the Assembly, the deputy for Trabzon could not be found anywhere in Ankara. He must have returned to his constituency, the authorities maintained: but there were rumours that Kemal's bodyguard had abducted him from the terrace of a café at the foot of the old citadel; and, five days later, what remained of Ali Shükru's body was found in a shallow grave close to Kemal's villa at Chankaya, five miles from the town centre.

Kemal placed the blame for Ali Shükru's death on the over-zealous Colonel of his bodyguard, Topal Osman, a sinister watchdog who in earlier years practised brigandage with some success in the mountains of the Black Sea coast. Osman, who was fanatically devoted to the Ghazi, mistrusted any spokesman for law and order in Trabzon, a district where, with good reason, the old brigand had many enemies. After the attack on Kemal's reputation, Topal Osman assumed that it was his duty to rid Ankara of Ali Shükru. Kemal at once realized that he must distance himself from Osman and the bodyguard. So ugly was the mood of the deputies that he left his villa and moved back to a building near the railway station which had been his headquarters during the Greek advance into Anatolia. A detachment of soldiery was sent to Chankaya, where Osman and some twenty of his old followers resisted them. There was a brief shoot-out; twelve of the bodyguard were killed and Osman mortally wounded. The Assembly, having adjourned its session to mark respect for the dead deputy for Trabzon, ordered the mutilated body of Topal Osman to be hung up outside the building so as to discourage other would-be assassins.

No one openly accused Kemal of ordering Ali Shükru's murder, but momentarily the whole episode shook his credibility as Turkey's newly discovered responsible modern statesman. Soon, however, he regained the political initiative. The First Grand National Assembly had sat for three years. It could be argued that, with the Sultan in exile and the final form of the Turkish state unresolved, it was time for new elections, to bring to Ankara deputies who recognized the need for progressive reforms. Accordingly, on 16 April 1923, the Assembly held its last session, the deputies either retiring from political life or preparing to canvass support in their constituencies. A week later, with no Assembly to criticize him, Ismet was back at Lausanne, carefully briefed on ways to convince the British and French that it was intolerable to expect a modern state to accept the loss of sovereignty implied by the hated Capitulations.

Ismet did well that summer. The Capitulations were abolished and it was agreed to leave the future of Mosul to arbitration by the League of Nations, although the province was provisionally incorporated in British-mandated Iraq. The Treaty of Lausanne was finally signed on 24 July 1923, the only World War I peace settlement to have been negotiated, rather than imposed by the victors. The Turks accepted the loss of the Ottoman Empire's Arab lands but they were confirmed in possession of eastern Thrace, Smyrna and its hinterland, the islands of Imbros and Tenedos, and the shores of both the Bosphorus and the Dardanelles, although there were to be demilitarized zones along the Thracian frontier and in the Straits. At the same time, the Treaty confirmed agreements already reached between the Turks and the Greeks for an exchange of population: slightly over a million Greeks were expelled from Asia Minor; and 350,000 Turks duly left Greece for their homeland. The Greek community remained large within Constantinople itself. But with the conclusion of the Treaty there would no longer be any foreign military presence on the Straits or in the historic capital; and General Harington and the last occupation troops left Constantinople in mid-September.

At first Ismet's success helped Kemal with his political problems at home. For the first time he organized his followers as a 'People's Party', pledged to uphold the National Pact. While the negotations were continuing in Lausanne, the Ghazi resumed travels in Asiatic Turkey which he had begun earlier in the year. He went, so he maintained, as a teacher, explaining the need for modernization to communities puzzled by a swiftly changing social scene. But the teacher was constantly learning as he travelled around. He found that, with the disappearance of old political forms, the townsfolk and villagers of Anatolia were clinging more and more to the familiar teachings of the Prophet, as expounded each Friday in the mosque. Even his proposal that the Friday sermons should be in vernacular Turkish rather than in Arabic aroused suspicion. Although the peasants welcomed his promises that the new Turkey would encourage farming and light rural industry, they listened anxiously for proof that the Ghazi was a true son of Islam, prepared to sustain the caliphate even if the sultanate had gone for all time. On the other hand, they recognized that diplomatic success at Lausanne was following the military victories against foreign invaders. A genuine pride in national identity made the peasants prepared to back the delegates he nominated as spokesmen for the People's Party. By mid-August 1923 the elections had returned a new and more tractable Assembly to Ankara. 'The Grand National Assembly embodies the essence of what the Turkish nation has been striving for throughout the centuries,' Kemal told the delegates. 'It is a living symbol of the nation's will for self-rule.'[5]

In that autumn Kemal proposed two reforms of deep significance. With Constantinople no longer occupied by foreign troops, there was every reason for the Assembly to return to the imperial capital. Such a move Kemal strongly opposed. Though a convinced Westernizer, his personal theory of history gloried in the Asian origins of the Turks; he was prepared to argue that when the Sultans crossed into Europe and ruled as Islamic successors to the Byzantine Emperors they were ensnared by their new acquisitions and fatally weakened. He therefore piloted a law through the Assembly in the second week of October which declared that 'the seat of the Turkish State is in Angora', thus confirming Ankara as the national capital. Plans were made for new avenues, administrative offices, a parliament building and, high in Kemal's list of priorities, an opera house. Foreign governments were expected to establish embassies, vacating their prestigious palaces and villas beside the Bosphorus. The diplomatic corps moved to central Anatolia with deep reluctance, and as slowly as possible.

Since most parliamentary deputies came from Anatolia they readily accepted the change of capital. By contrast, Kemal's second reform caused much heart-searching. For, with support from Fethi and Ismet, Kemal drafted a brief constitutional law declaring Turkey a republic, even though there was no republican sentiment in the Assembly and no precedent for a republic in Islam. The proposed reform provided for a president who would be elected by the Assembly and who would then appoint a prime minister. On the morning of 29 October the constitutional law was presented to a meeting of the People's Party executive; that evening it was hurried through an Assembly taken completely by surprise. One hundred and fifty-eight deputies duly voted for Kemal as president; no one else was nominated; but more than a hundred deputies abstained that evening. Ismet was appointed Prime Minister, Fethi became the nominal president of the Assembly (the equivalent of Speaker in the House of Commons or the House of Representatives). Yet effectively Kemal was Turkey's sole master, with more power in his hands than either Mussolini in Italy or the ailing Lenin in Russia.

There remained, of course, at the Dolmabahçe Palace in Constantinople a spiritual head, not only of Turkish believers, but of all Muslims. Caliph Abdul Mejid II was not personally unpopular, even though he thought it would be detrimental to his office to accept a simpler style of life than his predecessors enjoyed as both Caliph and Sultan. In February 1924 two prominent Muslims from the Indian sub-continent, Ameer Ali and the Aga Khan, wrote to Ismet urging the Turkish State to guarantee to the caliphate an international status, 'commanding the confidence and esteem of the Muslim peoples'. A copy of this letter was printed in a Turkish newspaper before it was officially received by the prime minister and its ill-considered words were exploited by Kemal and by the Turkish Press. The letter, they argued, proved that the caliphate was a potential source of outside interference in the affairs of the new republic. In a speech to the Assembly Kemal asked the deputies 'to enrich the Islamic religion' by liberating the faith from political control by an archaic institution; and on Monday, 3 March 1924, the deputies voted for the abolition of the caliphate and the deposition of Abdul Mejid. The Ministry of Religious Affairs was closed down and religious schools were placed under the supervision of the ministry of public instruction. All members of the fallen dynasty were forbidden to live within the Turkish republic.[6]

Abdul Mejid was awoken in his room at the Dolmabahçe soon after midnight and told he must leave the palace at five o'clock in the morning. A car sped him to Chatalja before news of his deposition broke in the newspapers. During the course of the day he was joined by numerous other members of the imperial family. There were no demonstrations for or against the Caliph; and on that Tuesday night the last of the Ottoman dynasty crossed the frontier of the republic aboard the Orient Express.

A month later the religious courts in Turkey were abolished, thus denying the right of Islamic Holy Law to resolve questions concerning not only marriage and divorce but claims of inheritance and other aspects of family life. It was announced that a civil code would eventually be promulgated to reconcile the different legal traditions. This secularization of the state was carried through with deceptive smoothness. It seemed as if the Turks, after all these years of war and upheaval, only wished to be allowed to till their fields and get the factories going again. But three founder members of the Turkish National Movement were uneasy at the course of events. Rauf had left the government while Ismet was at Lausanne for the final meetings of the conference. He remained a deputy, but had long absented himself from sessions of the Assembly. General Ali Fuad and General Kiazim Karabekir, too, were absentee deputies, both holding army commands away from the capital. However, in the early autumn of 1924 these three potential dissidents came together, meeting at Rauf's home in Sisli, then a north-western suburb of Constantinople. They agreed to support Kemal's policies but seek to slow down the pace of reform. The two generals resigned from the army and, with Rauf, took their seats in the Assembly. When they found that their advice and opinions counted for nothing within the People's Party they followed western European political precedent and withdrew their party membership. In the third week of November 1924, they announced the formation of an opposition pressure group which became known as the Progressive Republican Party. Some thirty deputies joined Ali Fuad, Rauf and Kiazim in the new party.[7]

At first Kemal was prepared to accept this step towards parliamentary democracy. When the deputies persisted in criticizing Ismet for the harsh conditions awaiting Turks repatriated from Greece under the terms of the Lausanne Treaty, he persuaded his prime minister to leave office on grounds of poor health. Fethi succeeded him. But tensions were too strained to favour a peaceful transition to democracy. After starting a brawl in one of the lobbies, an opposition deputy was shot dead by a member of the People's Party, against whom no action was taken because it was claimed he fired in self-defence. Fethi was more liberal than his predecessor and Kemal feared that he was losing control of the national revolution. When, in February 1925, south-eastern Turkey was shaken by a Kurdish revolt, the Ghazi used the threat of civil war to cajole the Assembly into conferring emergency powers on the government. Ismet returned to the premiership in the first week of March, determined to check the mounting unrest. 'Independence Tribunals' were established, comprised, for the most part, of People's Party deputies who were granted powers of summary execution and sent out 'to maintain public order' in remote regions of the republic as well as in Ankara and the larger towns of Anatolia. Their activities were reminiscent of the Jacobin commissions at the height of the French Revolution. Although no action was taken against leading Progressives, many of their follow-ers were intimidated; and the Progressive Republican Party was proscribed in June 1925, only thirty-two weeks after its foundation.

The Kurdish insurrection alarmed Kemal. Although the Kurds were a national minority striving for autonomy, this rebellion was provoked primarily by religious griev-ances; it therefore threatened to topple the secular republic which he was still building. The leader of the Kurds, Sheikh Said, unfurled the green banner of Islam, denounced Kemal as a godless imbiber of alcohol, and called for the restoration of the Caliphate and the full rigours of Islamic law. The rebellion, first reported on 11 February from the mountainous central region of Dersim, spread like a forest fire, swiftly engulfing the city of Elâziğ and isolating the garrison of Diyarbakir, where Kemal and Ismet had planned operations against the Russians eight

years before. Sheikh Said counted on support from one
of the dervish fraternities, the Nakshibendis, and hoped
that similar fanatical sectarians in south-western Turkey
would respond to his incitement of a holy war against the
Westernizer. In this, however, he failed; no other dervish
brotherhood was prepared to acknowledge the spiritual
leadership of Said or the Nakshibendis. Meticulously the
Turkish General Staff planned his encirclement, even
receiving permission from the French to move troops
along the railway south of the frontier in northern Syria.
By late March eight divisions were deployed across
Turkey's Kurdish lands, a wild region of blizzard-swept
mountains where the valleys provide the headwaters of
the Tigris and the Euphrates. Sheikh Said was captured
on 12 April and eventually brought before the Independence Tribunal in Diyarbakir. He had little doubt of his
fate. At the end of June, he was hanged, together with
nine other sheikhs and some thirty of their followers. Their
bodies were left suspended from gallows in the great
square outside Diyarbakir's eleventh-century Ulu Mosque
as a deterrent to other religious fanatics.[8]

Kemal was relieved that Sheikh Said's call to a holy
war had found no answer elsewhere in Turkey. It
confirmed his earlier intuitive feeling that most Turks
would remain indifferent to gradual secularization.
Already every mullah (religious teacher) and every
muezzin (prayer leader in the mosque) had to be regis-
tered and licensed by the Prime Minister's Directorate of
Religious Affairs, which controlled their payment and
could revoke their licence. After the threat from the
Kurdish dervishes had been contained, Kemal decided to
carry the secularist revolution even further: in early
September 1925 all dervish communities were
suppressed, and sacred tombs were closed as places of
worship. Kemal insisted that he was the enemy, not of
religious belief, but of Islamic clericalism.

At the same time, he was also determined to break the

influence of the old religious taboos on dress. On 25 August 1925 he set out by car from Ankara to travel 150 miles north-eastwards to Kastamonu wearing a light grey suit, open-necked shirt – and, on his head, a Panama. His five companions also carried hats: the fez was discarded as a symbol of the past, like the turban a century before. The people of Kastamonu took note of their president's attire, and were puzzled. Three days later Kemal reached the small Black Sea port of Inebolu, where as in Kastamonu, the word *shapka* (hat) was virtually an obscenity. But in his speech at Inebolu he declared:

'A civilized, cosmopolitan dress is worthy and fitting for our nation, and we will wear it – shoes on the feet, trousers on the legs, shirts with a tie under a collar, jackets and coats, and of course to go with all this, a headcovering with a brim for protection from the sun.'

And, pointing to his Panama, he continued:

'The name of this is "hat". There are those who say, "This is not permitted by sacred law." But I say to them, "You are very ignorant ... If wearing the fez, which is the old headgear of the Greeks, is permitted by Holy Law, why is not the wearing of a hat?"'

So far he had been speaking to the men. Now he turned to the women. They had, he said, been downtrodden in Turkey through the centuries; in a modern, civilized society they would enjoy emancipation:

'Male comrades, this is in part a consequence of our selfishness ... Our women are sensible, thinking people, as we are too ... Let them show their faces to the world. Let them be able to view the world with understanding. There is nothing to fear in all this.'[9]

Such startling remarks from their Head of State made a deep impression, not only in this backward region along the coast, but in other parts of Turkey, where the President's words were given prominence by the local newspapers. Photographs were printed of the Ghazi wearing his Panama and seated at the wheel of a farm tractor so that, when the more fortunate peasants sought to increase the yield of their fields, they, too, might aspire to drive the infidel's machinery and wear the infidel's hat. More immediate was the effect of Kemal's speech on the people of the capital. Nine days later when he returned to Ankara, he found that there had been a rush to buy hats or to improvise 'western' headgear; makers of Panamas became wealthy men overnight. But, though the fez might be discarded, the double-veiled yashmak of the Muslim women was not. The 'male comrades' were slow to react to the later part of the Ghazi's speech.

A series of decrees, issued under the Emergency Regulations imposed earlier in the year, soon enforced the sartorial revolution for men. The wearing of religious dress outside the mosques was strictly controlled; and in November the Assembly formally passed a law making the wearing of the fez a criminal offence. In some eastern towns and villages there was resistance to such impious regulations: the army and militia had to intervene, and lives were lost. Yet, while Turkish society was often being dragged into the twentieth century crudely and roughly, jurists were at work on a new legal system. They rejected the full Napoleonic structure, upon which French jurisprudence was still based, in favour of two variants: the civil code of Switzerland; and the penal code of Italy. A commercial code, based upon the business law of Germany, followed a few years later. 'The greatest, and at the same time the most insidious, enemies of [social] revolutionaries are rotten laws and their decrepit upholders,' Kemal declared in a speech on 5 November 1925, when he opened Ankara's first modern law school.[10] By February 1926 Turkey had an independent judiciary, civil marriage and divorce under a system of equal rights for both parties, and in theory the promise of unfettered professional opportunities for women.

Despite these impressive legal reforms the Independence Tribunals continued to serve as an intimidating political weapon for another thirteen months after the Assembly enacted Turkey's new civil code. In the summer of 1926 a plot to assassinate Kemal was revealed. The tale of the conspiracy reads at times like the synopsis of one of Shakespeare's medieval histories. A young naval officer from Tabzon, Ziya Hursid, had long harboured resentment towards the president because of the murder of his family friend, Ali Shükru, by Kemal's bodyguard, for he did not feel that the subsequent action against Topal Osman had cleared the Ghazi of complicity in the affair. At the same time Kemal's former friend, Colonel Arif, had a grievance: the Ghazi had excluded Arif from his circle of intimate cronies and denied him promotion because of a strong suspicion that he was growing rich through venal enterprises. Ziya met Arif and also several former members of the CUP who remained hostile to Kemal. The conspirators then hired three hit-men whom Ziya armed with revolvers and grenades and showed the best point for an assassination in the narrow streets of the old Muslim quarter of Izmir, as Smyrna was now called, where Kemal was expected at the end of the second week in June. The assassins in their turn found a Cretan refugee with a motor-boat who would help them escape. However, the Cretan thought he was being implicated by Turks who wished the blame to be placed on someone who had Greek connections; and he duly informed the provincial governor in Izmir. The would-be assassins were arrested and the origins of the plot traced back to Ziya and Arif. When Kemal arrived safely in Izmir, he personally interrogated Ziya, having discovered from secret police reports that he had contacts with several deputies in the Assembly and had sought support from the Progressives, although in vain.

There followed in July and August two much-publicized 'treason trials' before the Independence Tribunal, sitting first in a converted cinema at Izmir and later in Ankara. Among the alleged conspirators who were taken into custody were not only Ziya, Arif and their hit-men but also some prominent deputies. To the consternation of many veterans of the War of Independence, they included the former leading Progressives – Ali Fuad, Rauf, Kiazam Karabekir and Refet. Throughout the three-week trial at Izmir, Kemal stayed at Cesme, a small town fifty-five miles away, at the tip of the peninsula commanding the approaches to the Gulf. He was thus kept closely informed of all that was said in the cinema-courtroom and of public reaction to the arraignment of four 'founding fathers' of the Turkish Nationalist Movement. The principal conspirators were sentenced to death. Thirteen were publicly hanged in Izmir; among them was Arif, who until the last minute hoped that his old friendship with Kemal would win him a reprieve. Rauf and seven Progressives were either exiled or imprisoned. Sentences on a group of former CUP members were postponed because they were to be indicted on a further charge in Ankara. But Ali Fuad, Kiazam Karabekir, Refet, two other Generals and ten Progressives were acquitted and set free, amid widespread acclamation. Kemal was left in no doubt that the arrest of such distinguished soldiers on trumped-up charges was unpopular with many ordinary Turks, the people on whom he counted for support. A year later there was a somewhat frigid rapprochement between Kemal and Ali Fuad, but the other acquitted men – and those sent into exile – took no further part in political or military affairs until after the Ghazi's death.

The Ankara trial, before the same two judges of the Independence Tribunal, began on 1 August 1926 and dragged on for twenty-six days. Over forty men were accused, not of planning Kemal's assassination, but of anti-government activities. Among their offences were alleged links with Enver before 1922, when he was killed by the Red Army in an obscure cavalry skirmish in Turkestan. One leading Young Turks survivor, Mehmed Djavid (minister of finance in 1914), was sentenced to death for treason and, with three alleged conspirators against the state, was publicly hanged in the main square of old Ankara. In contrast to the treason trials of Stalin's Russia, thirty-seven of the accused were acquitted. But the lesson of the Turkish trials was that, however much Kemal might pay lip-service to an ideal of democracy, opposition was dangerous and intrigue foolhardy.[11]

In 1924 Kemal had sailed through the Dardanelles and the Bosphorus without setting foot in Constantinople, where he believed he still had too many political enemies. After the treason trials, however, he felt more secure. The Independence Tribunal was formally abolished in March 1927, and a few weeks later he instructed his sister, Makbule, to supervise the preparation of a presidential suite in a wing of the Dolmabahçe Palace, for after an absence of more than eight years, he intended to return to the city, which by now all Turks called Istanbul. He left Ankara on 30 June in a beflagged train, embarked on *Ertügrül*, the former royal yacht of the Sultans, at Izmit and landed at the palace quay to the sounds of great cheering from the crowd along the waterfront and to the echo of naval salutes. Days of celebration were followed by a procession of ships of all types passing up the Bosphorus and in front of the broad marble terrace of the Dolmabahçe. 'I have returned to a smiling and flourishing Istanbul,' Kemal declared in reply to a speech of welcome from the Mayor. 'Istanbul, standing where two great worlds come together, is the treasure of Turkish history, the cherished jewel of the Turkish nation, a city with a place in the hearts of all our countrymen.'[12]

He remained in residence at the Dolmabahçe until the

early autumn, working hard at an unfamiliar task. For now that he had returned to the old capital he wished the Turkish people to see their National Revolution as a fact of history. Much reconstruction work remained to be completed – on the status of women, on basic education, on the growth of industry and agriculture, and perhaps ultimately in shaping a stable democracy – but he could legitimately claim to have changed drastically the form and character of the Turkish homeland in less than a decade. Now he intended to present his own account of the Revolution to the Congress of the People's Party, which was to meet in Ankara in October. Characteristically he decided to do so in a speech; for, like Hitler, he always believed that the spoken word wins more followers than the written word. Nevertheless, he had every intention of having the speech printed, translated and circulated throughout the world. It should serve as his political testament, a guide to the past and a pointer to the future.

This 'Great Speech', on which he began work in mid-July, was a thoroughly documented but highly selective account of what he wished remembered of the eight years after 'I landed at Samsun on 19 May 1919'. One of his secretaries recalled, half a century later, how Kemal would work almost without stopping, sometimes for as long as twenty-four hours at a stretch, subsisting mainly on coffee and cigarettes; he would take no alcohol whatsoever while he was engaged in such concentrated activity. Three sets of secretaries were employed, either taking dictation in shorthand or transcribing what he had himself jotted down on pads of paper. Friends were summoned to his presence to listen to particular sections after the secretaries had typed them out for him. Revision continued week after week, and the speech was not finished until he returned to Ankara.[13]

The Congress of the People's Party opened on Saturday, 15 October 1927, in that cramped single-storeyed building which was the Grand National Assembly's home for the first four years of its existence. Kemal addressed party members for six hours on each of the six days, finally sitting down to what must have been particularly thankful applause on the following Thursday afternoon. When the earliest English-language version was published in Leipzig two years later it was printed in a single volume of 724 pages, with some 400 words to the page. Although less than fair to Rauf, Ali Fuad, Kiazim or any of the Progressives, the speech at last placed in perspective the achievements of the Revolution against a background of the War of Independence. Yet it was only in the last hour of his delivery that Kemal's prime objective became clear. For he knew that, in a country in which the population was rising rapidly, he had to win and hold the next generation. After the long chronicle of past deeds he therefore addressed his peroration to 'Turkish Youth': their 'primary duty must be the preservation and defence of national independence in the Turkish Republic', a task made possible, 'O Turkish child of the future', by the strength 'which flows from the noble blood in your veins.'[14] Fine words for a crisis which Kemal hoped would never shake the nation. For increasingly he sought escape from the role of warrior hero, appearing less and less in full uniform. Turkish youth should see him as a father figure, their wise and modern teacher who was also a guarantor of peace and stability.

Father Turk 5

When Kemal returned to Istanbul in the summer of 1927
as the revered president of the young republic, there was
no First Lady to share with him the popular acclamation.
He had left the Sultan's capital in 1919 deeply attached to
his kinswoman Fikriye, the niece of Zubeyde's second
husband. But at Smyrna in September 1922 he was fascinated by Latife, a highly sophisticated twenty-four-year-
old who was the much cherished daughter of Ushakizade
Muammer, a Turkish businessman in the city. Latife had
completed her education in Paris; she spoke French
fluently and some English. Although she still wore a traditional head covering, she had long since discarded her
veil. When the Great Fire threatened Kemal's headquarters, he moved to her father's impressive villa at
Gozetepe, along the coast, where Latife was a naturally
gracious hostess at the dinner table. It seemed to Kemal
that he had found a prototype of the ideal twentieth-
century woman – elegant, self-assured but dutiful, someone who was even ready to peruse and summarize
newspapers for him at breakfast. At his dictation Latife
was able to write, in English, a virtual ultimatum to
General Harington during the crisis at Chanak. She was

willing to flirt with Kemal but not become his mistress, for she had every intention of making him her husband.

That, too, remained the ambition of Fikriye. In June 1921 Kemal had brought Fikriye to Ankara, at her own request, to serve as his housekeeper in the home he was about to create on the hillside at Chankaya. Fikriye had never lived outside the Ottoman Empire, but in Macedonia she had acquired some 'western' social accomplishments. She was a good horsewoman, creating a minor sensation when she galloped through the dusty streets of Ankara. But Fikriye could also play the piano, and she was prepared to dress in a skirt and blouse. The Ghazi's personal staff readily accepted her as châtelaine of Chankaya, even when she was joined in December by Kemal's septuagenarian mother. Zubeyde was proud of Kemal, although pained by his contempt for Islamic tradition. She liked Fikriye but maintained that she was not suited to become his wife as she had been married once already, to an Egyptian; Muslim convention assumed that a Pasha would take as his first wife a chaste virgin. Kemal treated Fikriye with an almost brotherly affection; he scoffed at his mother's objections but, at the same time, had no intention of according the Macedonian refugee high status in his new Turkey, however devoted she might be to him. Early hardship weakened Fikriye's health. When she developed tuberculosis Kemal arranged for her to receive treatment in Swiss and German sanatoria. He also sent Zubeyde away from Ankara, sparing his mother the rigours of an Anatolian winter by despatching her to stay at Latife's family villa in Gozetepe. There she was treated with great honour as the mother of Turkey's national saviour. But poor Zubeyde was unhappy; she was uncomfortable in such mock-Riviera luxury; she pined for the simplicity of life she had known for more than a third of a century in Salonika. Within a month of arriving at Gozetepe, her health gave way; before her son could complete his journey from

Ankara, she was dead. A fortnight later – on 29 January 1923 – Kemal married Latife in Izmir.

Several close companions of the Ghazi had heard Zubeyde express doubts whether 'this Western lady' whom she came to know at Gozetepe could 'make my Mustafa happy.' Her fears were justified: their union lasted for less than a thousand days. Latife had been a discreet hostess before her marriage but, as wife to the President, she was determined to change her husband's social habits. She particularly disliked the long hours he would spend drinking raki or enjoying poker with his cronies. Kemal's genuine encouragement of women's emancipation in public life was, at home, limited by his pride as head of a household. Implied rebukes by his young wife in front of other men angered him. At twenty-five the fascinating Latife had become a scold.

No less disturbing to Kemal's concept of an idealized husband and wife relationship was the impact of a personal tragedy which he found hard to understand. Fikriye learned of his marriage from glancing at a newspaper being read by a fellow patient in her Munich sanatorium. She returned at once to Ankara, and stayed as a guest of Kemal and Latife for four days at Chankaya in the early summer of 1923, but she found life there so impossible that she moved to a hotel in the capital. When, a few days later, Fikriye sought to return to the presidential residence, she was refused admission. As she was being driven in a carriage back to her hotel, she shot herself with a revolver she had purchased in Germany; she died in hospital. Any guilt which Kemal may have felt over Fikriye's suicide he turned against Latife, but the couple did not separate for another couple of years. After a shrewdly negotiated personal settlement, the marriage was dissolved on 5 August 1925. Latife withdrew into quiet private life in Istanbul, a city from which she would discreetly absent herself if the Ghazi came into residence at the Dolmabaçhe. She outlived him by thirty-eight years.[1]

His experiences with Fikriye and Latife made Kemal disinclined to take another wife. His sister, Makbule, who never married, managed such domestic affairs as he did not leave to his personal staff. Nevertheless he became increasingly isolated, especially when a year after his divorce the Izmir assassination plot and the treason trials marked a break with many former companions. Kemal remained on good terms with a small circle of trusted friends: Salih, an aide-de-camp whom he had first known in Salonika; Kilic Ali, a cavalry officer with whom he enjoyed riding down to the model farm he created at Ankara; and Ali Fethi, who was however absent from Turkey from 1925 to 1930, serving as ambassador in Paris. Even before the divorce of Latife – and to her intense disapproval – Kemal renewed acquaintance with Nuri, a classmate from Salonika who served under him in the Gallipoli peninsula. Kemal and Nuri would hunt Angora rabbits on the hills around the capital in the early morning, before inducing Nuri's wife to provide them with a breakfast of sesame and molasses, a favourite dish of both men in their Macedonian boyhood.

In the company of Nuri, and his wife and children, Kemal would relax happily and quite naturally. But there were other occasions when relaxation was imposed artificially, as part of a process of enforced Westernization. In Paris in 1910 and during his brief term of duty in Sofia Kemal was impressed by the social splendour of the audience at the opera, and two decades later the legislators and bureaucrats of Ankara found themselves expected to show enthusiasm for the opera house which he built half a mile from the railway station. They were not required to like opera itself – the Ghazi's standard of appreciation was based on a whistling acquaintance with Bizet's *Carmen* – but they had to attend, impeccably dressed, on gala occasions. Yet it would be wrong to suggest that Kemal's cultural outlook was philistine. Familiarity with classical music seemed to Kemal socially desirable. By the mid-1930s a State Conservatory was flourishing in Ankara, under the joint direction of the German refugee Paul Hindemith, and the Turkish violinist Licco Amar. Kemal would have been especially gratified at the high standards reached after his death by Turkish ballet companies, for he spent many evenings seeking to convince would-be 'modern' Turks that dance was a graceful form of cultural development which might be enjoyed and expressed by women of good society.[2]

Long before Kemal was accepted as the saviour of the nation, he had become accustomed to playing a father-figure role in an extended family. In Macedonia, there had been poor Fikriye and her sister who died young. They had been joined in Istanbul by a three-year-old orphan boy from the Balkan Wars, Abdurrahim, who was a dutiful companion for Zubeyde in her later years. Abdurrahim's origins are obscure; he later trained as an engineer in Germany and, in middle age, bore a facial resemblance to his foster-father, Kemal. While still in Istanbul, Zubeyde also had entrusted to her by Kemal a war-orphan girl, Afife. Seven more adopted daughters became young companions for him at Ankara: most were adolescents, but the last – Ülkü, a toddler of whom he was particularly fond – was the child of a servant in the presidential home and the station-master at the railway halt for his model farm. The girls lived, for the most part, at Chankaya, where they received special schooling.[3]

Foreign diplomats and other outsiders inevitably believed that Turkey's ruler was establishing a revamped harem at Chankaya. This assumption was unduly simplistic. Afet, the eldest 'daughter', was a beautiful, serious-minded young woman who later married and became a historian. During the last years of Kemal's life she accepted the responsibilities of head of his household, and was a patient and understanding companion for him. Kemal was interested in moulding the minds and shaping the careers of the girls, hoping that they would become exemplars of 'the modern Turkish woman', emancipated, responsible and law-abiding. He demanded too high a level of excellence of one daughter, who fell from a train in France while returning to Ankara after several months of study in England. But other daughters fulfilled their foster-father's expectations: one became a judge; another married a Turkish diplomat and created a great impression in Vienna before the Anschluss; and a third married a young army officer with a distinguished career ahead of him. Best known of these daughters was Sabiha, in 1925 a twelve-year-old orphan at Bursa where she caught Kemal's eye. On hearing from the child that she wished to leave home and go to boarding school, he induced her elder brother to allow her to join the presidential family at Chankaya. Eleven years later Sabiha graduated from the Military Air Academy as Turkey's pioneer woman pilot.

Kemal first sought to teach the nation by example in August 1925, when he set out on his 'The name of this is "hat"' speech-making campaign. Even more revolutionary was his decision in July 1928 to appoint a commission responsible for preparing a new alphabet, so that the Turkish language might be expressed in the Roman script of western Europe rather than in an Arabic form. Ultimately he intended to have the language modernized and simplified, ridding it of Ottoman court archaisms and of Arabic and Persian words and phrases. He was, however, convinced that if a new alphabet preceded linguistic reforms, it would help combat illiteracy. Ismet, as prime minister, agreed with Kemal. A change of alphabet was perfectly feasible, Ismet told him, although it would take seven years of gradual education before the new script could be used. The commission's chairman was more optimistic; five years, he thought. But these estimates did not match Kemal's intentions. Curtly he informed the government ministers and the commission that the change must be made before the end of the year, preferably within three months.

As in the previous summer Kemal left Ankara at the end of July 1928 and went into residence at the Dolma-bahçe Palace, beside the Bosphorus. On the evening of Friday, 9 August, a fête sponsored by the People's Party was held on the promontory of Sarayburnü. There were two bands to entertain the crowd, one playing modern jazz and the other competing with it by offering traditional music, with songs in Arabic by Egyptian vocalists. The bands fell silent, as the Ghazi rose to deliver a sensational speech. When he did so, it was to instruct the crowd 'in the new Turkish letters with which our rich and harmonious language will now be able to display itself'. At the end of a peroration which denounced the hypocrisy of the Ottoman rulers who would drink in secret while outwardly insisting on maintenance of the Islamic ban on alcohol, Kemal lifted a glass full of raki and proposed a toast 'to the honour of my nation'.[4] Ismet, who encouraged the idea of the Ghazi as 'the headmaster of the Turkish people', was uneasy at such a staged and unconventional approach, especially on a Muslim day of prayer. Yet there were many onlookers at Sarayburnü who followed Kemal's example with enthusiasm. For them, the painful process of learning a new alphabet was associated with modern jazz and freedom to drink openly. No doubt it was a less successful evening for the Egyptian vocalists.

A few days later 'Turkey's headmaster' had black-boards put up in the old audience chamber and reception halls of the Dolmabahçe Palace. He personally gave lessons explaining the new Turkish alphabet to delegations who came to the Palace and, indeed, to ministers, deputies and civil servants. It was a task he enjoyed so much that he carried the work further afield, travelling down to Tekirdag on the European shore of the Sea of Marmara a fortnight after the Sarayburnü fête. There he gave a two-hour lesson in the open air. Later he crossed the Bosphorus to give lessons at Kadikoi, Izmit, Bursa and other towns and villages in western Anatolia. Photographs of Kemal at one of his blackboards were circulated throughout the country. When he returned to Ankara, public buildings were fitted with lights in which the new alphabet was displayed after dark. It was imposed on the country by law on 3 November, becoming obligatory on New Year's Day 1929. Almost at the same time – on 11 November – the Grand National Assembly proclaimed that, in the battle for literacy, 'the whole Turkish nation was a school', with 'His Excellency the President of the Republic' as 'chief instructor'.[5] By the end of the year 1929 a million children and illiterates – about one in sixteen of the total population – had learned how to read by this intensive course of education in the new alphabet. Kemal was well-satisfied with the progress of the reform.

Theoretically he still believed in democracy, even though he forced changes upon Turkey as imperiously as any autocratic Sultan. When, in the summer of 1930, Fethi returned to Turkey from his term as ambassador in Paris, he discussed with Kemal the possibility of encouraging the growth of a 'loyal opposition' in the Assembly, if only as a safety-valve for deputies with a grievance. Accordingly, in the second week of August 1930, Kemal accepted the principle of two-party government: the old 'People's Party' – now known as the 'Republican People's Party' (RPP) – would be faced by a Free Republican Party, with Fethi as chairman. Kemal's friend Nuri became secretary and Kemal's sister Makbule was a founder member. Unlike the ill-fated Progressives six years before, the new Free Party, as it was called, received official blessing from the start.

In 1924–25 the first experiment in two-party government lasted less than nine months; this second experiment survived for nine weeks.[6] When Fethi held public meetings in Anatolia he found feeling hardening against the Ghazi's irreligious reforms. Fethi, who was in many ways more progressive than Ismet or Kemal himself, discovered to his surprise that the only welcome alternative to RPP policies was a rural conservatism. To his consternation, the green flag of Islam was waved at Free Party meetings by fanatics with whom he had nothing in common. In the Grand National Assembly he was faced by a totally different problem. For when, early in November, Fethi sought to move a vote of censure on a government minister whom he accused of corruption, he became a victim of such impassioned personal abuse that his life seemed in danger. Rather than risk anarchy in the Assembly, Fethi and Nuri readily agreed with Kemal that the Free Party should be dissolved. A number of nominally 'independent' deputies – perhaps as many as a dozen – were returned to the Grand National Assembly of 1935, but their task was to criticize details of legislation, not basic policy. Twelve years passed before a more successful attempt was made to organize a licensed opposition. By then Kemal was dead.

The green flags at Free Party meetings showed that Islamic tradition was still an active force. Less than seven weeks after the party was dissolved religious fanaticism exploded in a riot, not in the troubled eastern outback, but at Menemem, in the Aegean coastal region north of Izmir. During midday prayers on 23 December 1930 a group of Nakshibendi dervishes, led by a rabble-rouser known as Sheikh Mehmen, called on the faithful to follow them out of the mosque and destroy every symbol of Kemal's new Turkey, the godless republic that had dared to abolish the fez, the women's veil and the Arabic script. In the main square of Menemem the dervishes were confronted by a small detachment of troops under Lieutenant Mustafa Kubilay. They seized the young officer whom they decapitated with a hack-saw, carrying his head on a pole in the hopes of rousing the mob to rebellion. Prompt action by the Izmir garrison quelled the riot before it could spread elsewhere. Mehmen was captured;

together with many of his dervish supporters, he was put on trial for treason and executed. But the terrible fate of Kubilay, an officer who idolized Kemal and who fervently believed in Westernization, emphasized the depth of feeling over the religious question.[7]

The Menemem riot enabled Ismet to convince Kemal of the need to slow down social reform. At the same time, greater attention was given to explaining what the Ghazi was seeking to achieve. Kemal himself went on the radio, and in every sizeable town a 'People's House' was set up to serve, in part as a cultural institution, but also as a propaganda information office. A Turkish historical society was founded in 1931 to explain the nation's past in terms proudly relevant to the present; and it was followed a year later by another instrument of government-sponsored enlightenment, the Turkish language society. On the other hand, the further extension of women's rights was approached with particular caution. Not until December 1934 did the Grand National Assembly amend the basic constitution so as to give the vote to every Turkish man and woman over the age of twenty-three and allow women as well as men to be returned to the Assembly as deputies, provided they were at least thirty-one years old. On paper, from the beginning of 1935, Turkish women enjoyed full civic rights and equal opportunity in every branch of public life. Kemal's adopted daughter Afet was encouraged to write a history of the movement for Turkish women's social and political emancipation.

Kemal was no economist. From the first days of the national struggle he railed against European 'colonialism' which had given Germany, Great Britain, France and Italy a powerful grip on the pre-war Ottoman Empire; and the liquidation of foreign economic concessions became a dominant principle of early Kemalism. At the same time he wished to initiate a programme of extensive industrialization, concentrating in particular on the development of mineral resources. Only the mines and heavy industry were to be state-owned. But Turkey was economically so backward that industrialization required wise and undoctrinaire planning, backed by a sound banking system. Kemal was unable to provide leadership of this kind. Priority was, rightly, given to electrification of regions where it was hoped to build factories. When the Turkish Republic was proclaimed in 1923 there were only two electricity generating stations in the whole of the country; by 1930 there were fifty-six. Since more than three-quarters of the working population were directly dependent on the land, attempts were made to promote a factory system closely linked to the needs of agriculture, where cotton and tobacco were the chief crops. Four state-owned sugar-beet factories were opened in 1927, the largest of them at Eskişehir, but for several years it cost the Turks twice as much to produce sugar at home as to import it. Most crops came from Thrace or the coastal plains of Anatolia and low rainfall sometimes caused the failure of the harvest, as in 1929. This particular disaster was exacerbated by the effects of the world slump following the Wall Street crash in October of that year. Unlike western and central Europe, there was no urban unemployment in Kemal's Turkey; the town population remained small, except in Istanbul (where the Westernized clothing industry was creating new jobs); but in 1930 there was real suffering in the countryside. Although the protest movement at Free Party meetings that year might outwardly be concerned with Kemal's 'godlessness', the root cause of discontent was rural poverty. Significantly, during that summer banditry resurfaced along the Black Sea littoral and in eastern Anatolia for the first time in ten years.

Prime Minister Ismet favoured the state encouragement of industry and was a firm believer in opening up the interior by laying down thousands of miles of railway track. But, like Kemal, he had no overall strategic plan for

the economy, which continued to suffer from high indus-
trial and low agricultural prices, from dear credit, and
from the paucity of mechanized equipment. In June 1930
Turkey defaulted on the foreign debts which were a
legacy of the Ottoman Empire. In this crisis Kemal
imposed upon Ismet a financial wizard in whom he had
great confidence, Mahmud Jelâl – generally known by his
later name, Celâl Bayar. Already he had used money
contributed by rich Indian Muslim potentates to form the
first specifically Turkish bank in Ankara. This institution
survived the economic blizzard, an achievement which in
itself justified Celâl's appointment as Minister of Economic
Affairs.

Ismet resented Celâl's advancement, mistrusted his
insistence on heavy indirect taxation and high protective
tariffs, and showed little faith in his abilities. Ismet was
proved wrong. Between 1929 and 1939 the area of land
under cultivation doubled, but it was through the encouragement of industrialization and the exploitation of
Turkey's mineral resources that Celâl made his main
contribution to Turkey's well-being. Like Kemal and
Ismet, he abhorred communism and had no wish to see
the Soviet Union became a powerful neighbour, but he
was prepared to exploit the Russians and even follow
Stalin's precedent in re-ordering the economy through
state-planning.

In January 1934 Kemal backed Celâl's ambitious First
Five-Year Plan: Turkey was to have a huge steelworks at
Karabük, on the railway due north of Ankara but close to
the Black Sea harbours of Erĕgli and Zonguldak, where
there were coal mines; a textile industry was to be built
up around Nazilli in the Menderes plain and at Kayseri
(formerly Caesarea), the capital of Cappadocia, where an
aircraft factory was also established; Izmir, when fully
rebuilt after the fire, was to have paper mills and factories for producing cardboard and cellulose; and there
were to be new mills in Bursa and Adana. The most inter-

esting feature of the five-year plan was the dispersal of these industries over a huge area in Asia Minor, greater in extent than inter-war Germany. The Karabük enterprise was built by an English company, the funding guaranteed by the British government; and a substantial loan was negotiated, on good terms, with the Russians for textile machinery; but otherwise the cost of the five-year plan was met by taxation. A Turkish Central Bank and a Sumerian Bank were set up, in order to finance new ventures. When a second five-year plan was under discussion early in 1938 Kemal – by then a sick man – waived his old objection to contracting foreign loans with the 'colonialist' West and allowed Celâl to borrow £16 million from Great Britain, of which £6 million was to be spent on arms contracts with British firms. The Second Five-Year Plan was adopted in September 1938 and was followed by another large foreign loan, negotiated with Germany only a few weeks before Kemal's death. By then Nazi Germany was the recipient of more than half of Turkey's total exports.[8]

While, during the early 1930s, Celâl and Ismet were seeking to stabilize Turkey's economy, Kemal encouraged the gradual emergence of the republic from the self-imposed international isolationism which had followed the Treaty of Lausanne. He favoured accords with France and Great Britain, provided that successive governments in Paris and London would treat Turkey as an independent nation-state rather than as a dependent client. As early as 1921 the French recognized the legitimate concern of Kemal's government for the Turkish population of the Hatay, the northernmost province of French-mandated Syria, around Alexandretta; thereafter Franco–Turkish relations remained friendly. But delineation of the frontier with British-mandated Iraq at first imposed a strain on relations with London. The Lausanne Treaty had contemplated the inclusion within Iraq of the former Ottoman *vilayet* of Mosul, subject to League of

Nations approval. Despite the patriotic indignation of some hot-headed deputies in the Assembly, Kemal was prepared to lose the former *vilayet*, as the population was mainly Arab rather than Turk, but when in 1925 the British claimed a frontier further to the north, Kemal threatened war along the Tigris; he hurriedly concluded a non-aggression pact with the Soviet Union so as to withdraw troops from Turkey's eastern border. However, in June 1926 a treaty was signed in Ankara between Great Britain, Iraq and Turkey which settled the frontier along the northern border of the old *vilayet*; the Turks were promised compensation for the loss of oil revenue from the *vilayet*. That Kemal eventually accepted the astonishingly low settlement of £500,000 shows how earnestly he wished for better relations with London.

When, in 1932, Turkey sought to join the League of Nations, Kemal's application for membership was successfully backed by both the French and the British. To some extent, this support was a response to Turkey's growing mistrust of Italy and, in particular, of Mussolini's fortification of Rhodes and Léros in the Dodecanese. The Duce's professed ambitions in the eastern Mediterranean even brought Greece and Turkey together in a pact of friendship, with Kemal's old enemy Venizelos travelling to Ankara in October 1930 and joining the Ghazi on the saluting base at a military parade to honour Republic Day. Proposals that Kemal might travel to Greece, perhaps even returning to his birthplace, came to nothing – after the end of World War I he never once left Turkey. But Ismet, despite fears that he would be assassinated, bravely responded to Venizelos's courtesy by making an official visit to Athens. A Greco–Turkish Entente, unthinkable in the first years of the republic, was carefully nurtured by Kemal and Ismet a decade later.

In a gesture intended both to appease the Greeks and to assert his own secularism, Kemal gave notice that the great Byzantine cathedral of St Sophia must close as a mosque; and in 1932 restoration work began, as a preliminary to its reopening in 1934 as a national museum. The Greeks, who would have welcomed the return of Christian worship to St Sophia's, were not particularly impressed. More effective was Kemal's backing for a treaty in September 1933 which guaranteed the inviolability of the Greek–Turkish frontier and held out the prospect of mutual assistance in case of attack. This agreement was followed in February 1934 by a Balkan Pact, linking Greece, Turkey, Yugoslavia and Romania. Although the Pact served primarily as a 'Hands Off Thrace' warning to Bulgaria, it was also an anti-Italian gesture.

Kemal despised Mussolini as a caricature Caesar, but he recognized that in the early 1930s Italy could concentrate stronger air, military and naval forces in the eastern Mediterranean than any other Great Power. On 18 March 1934 a flamboyant speech by Mussolini, declaring that Italy's historic objectives lay in Asia and Africa, convinced Kemal that the Duce was about to launch a war similar to the conflict which had provided him with a baptism of fire in Libya almost a quarter of a century before. When, a year later, Mussolini began his imperialist ventures with the invasion of Ethiopia, Kemal argued that Turkey must look to the defence of Asia. With careful prompting from the British, the Turks avoided any unilateral action but sought, through the League of Nations, the revision of those clauses in the Lausanne settlement which had demilitarized the Dardanelles and Bosphorus. In July 1936 a convention signed at Montreux in Switzerland allowed Kemal to move troops back into the Straits, which became once again the great Turkish waterway.

Soon afterwards work began on the refortification of the Dardanelles. It was undertaken, however, not by Krupps of Essen, who supplied the original German guns and tendered the lowest estimate for the new work, but by the British armaments firm, Vickers. Kemal was convinced that Hitler intended to plunge Europe into another war and he was determined to avoid the mistakes of Enver and the Young Turks, who had become disastrously dependent upon the Kaiser's Germany. In the volume of memoirs entitled *Facing the Dictators*, Anthony Eden recalls how, in the summer of 1937, Kemal was so impressed by a British naval flotilla which 'flew the flag' in Turkish waters that he wished to have 'two cruisers and three destroyers' constructed 'in British yards exactly similar to those he had seen' off Istanbul.[9] The flagship of the Turkish navy in 1937 – and long afterwards – was still the *Yavuz*, launched at Hamburg in 1909 as the battle-cruiser *Goeben*.

A close partnership with Great Britain made good strategic sense in the mid-thirties, and after the conclusion of the Montreux Convention Kemal's Turkey was regarded in London as a focus of stability both for southeastern Europe and the Levant. The improved relationship between the two countries owed much to the shrewd diplomacy of Sir Percy Loraine who, as British ambassador in Ankara from 1933 onwards, became a personal friend of Kemal and one of his poker-table intimates at Chankaya. From the despatches which Sir Percy sent to the Foreign Office, he seems to have understood Kemal's fears, foibles and vanities better than any other Englishman.[10]

Sir Percy Loraine realized, in particular, the importance which Kemal attached to visits from eminent foreign dignitaries, among them the rulers of Yugoslavia, Iraq and Iran and the Chief-of-Staff of the US army, General MacArthur. In February 1936 Loraine had hopes that Winston Churchill would make the journey to Ankara. In this he was disappointed; but six months later his persistence in pressing for a prestigious British visit was rewarded, for, in the first week of September 1936, King Edward VIII was persuaded to pay a courtesy call on

Kemal at the Dolmabaçhe Palace in Istanbul while cruising with Mrs Simpson and other friends in the yacht *Nahlin*. Although both the ambassador and the President would have preferred the King to travel to Ankara rather than the old capital, Kemal was pleased to entertain the uncrowned King-Emperor in the last Sultan's palace and, on the following day, aboard the last Sultan's imperial yacht, for it was the first occasion upon which a reigning British monarch had visited Turkey. Although the President is alleged to have remarked in private that the King's infatuation with Mrs Simpson would cost him his throne, both Heads of State were well pleased with the courtesies they exchanged on the Bosphorus. Edward VIII (who reigned for only three more months) caught the magnetism of his host's personality, while the King's habitual ease of manner satisfied Kemal's belated Anglophilia.[11]

Thirteen years separated Kemal and Edward VIII in age, but photographs taken during the visit make the difference seem more like thirty. For, at fifty-five, the president looked prematurely old. In 1920–21 the defenders of Anatolia had become accustomed to the sight of their commander-in-chief, draped in a light grey great-coat, a slim figure with his face strained and ashen and piercingly cold eyes which seemed almost the same colour as his uniform. To boost morale during these gravest weeks of the War of Independence his supporters in the National Movement appropriated a famous Turkish legend, the tale of a nomadic tribe which found itself trapped in a valley. How the tribe came there or how they were to leave, nobody knew. Year after year the tribesmen stayed in the valley, unaware of life beyond the encircling mountains but multiplying there until there was no longer food or water to sustain them. In that desperate hour, a grey wolf suddenly appeared – alone, fierce and proudly unapproachable; the animal's nose pointed a way out which no one had seen before:

the threatened tribe followed the grey wolf safely
through a narrow pass and into the wider world.[12]

Kemal was long content to be identified as the
fabulous Grey Wolf. However, with the coming of stability
to the republic he sought a different image, for he could
no longer claim to be the sleek animal of the revolutionary years. In 1934 the Grand National Assembly had
approved a law which required Turks to take surnames
for the first time. Many military heroes chose to
commemorate victorious campaigns; thus General Ismet
became Ismet Inönü. Some took the names of rivers
associated with their earlier life, like Menderes or Aras. In
several instances the names were decided by Kemal
himself: his faithful friend Fethi was given the surname
Okyar ('companion in spirit') and the most intrepid of his
adopted daughters became Sabiha Gokcen ('Sabiha of
the Skies'). The President had no wish to go down in
posterity as the 'Grey Wolf'; nor did he choose to remember any one of his battles more than another. He
discarded his old first name Mustafa as an Arabic aber-
ration, retained the Kemal by which he was best remembered (though he hoped it would be spelt Kamal, a 'pure'
Turkish version); and on 29 November 1934 he finally
selected as a surname Atatürk – 'Father Turk'. Three
weeks later a special law forbade anyone else to use the
name, or any variation of it, although his sister Makbule
was permitted to take the surname Atadan ('related to
the father'). For the last four years of his life the president signed himself, quite simply, 'K. Atatürk'. But if
people addressed him as Atam ('My Father') he did not
rebuke them. Other twentieth-century dictators strutted
before their compatriots as uniformed leaders of a nation
state – Il Duce, Der Führer, El Caudillo. Kemal, who saw
no reason to dress as a soldier so long as the republic
was at peace, preferred the concept of guiding a nation
family towards maturity. The distinction, though subtle, is
valid – and revealing.

Apotheosis 6

When, as Dukē of Windsor in 1951, King Edward VIII published his memoirs he recalled one striking impression of the meetings with Kemal Atatürk: 'His eyes were the most piercing I have ever looked into,' the Duke wrote.[1] It was a feature upon which others who visited the president in Ankara and Istanbul also commented. Some of his compatriots believed that Atatürk possessed hypnotic powers, for there was something compelling about that steely blue gaze beneath the quizzical eyebrows, as concentrated as a ray of light. More prosaically, two ambassadors suggested independently of each other that the President liked 'no nonsense' conversations: 'One came to be able to translate that look,' Sir Percy Loraine wrote. 'It meant don't shilly-shally. We speak as man to man.'[2]

There was good reason for Kemal's liking for down-to-earth conversations. Habits that had weakened governments under the sultans of Turkey and tsars of Russia persisted long after the fall of the old autocracies; fear or flattery tended to make a ruler's intimate circle conceal unpleasant truths in the belief that cherished illusions, firmly held, guaranteed a happier and more contented

107

daily life. After March 1935, when the Grand National Assembly automatically re-elected Kemal for a fourth-year term as President of the Republic, he began to suspect that this familiar process of honouring the Head of State was increasingly insulating him from reality. More than once he 'escaped' from the Dolmabahçe Palace, to the consternation of his guards; even out at Chankaya he complained of being a prisoner of his official duties. When Nuri Conker died in January 1937 he lost contact, not only with a nostalgic past, but with a family whom he could observe making the transition from the old to the new Turkey. Falih Rifki Atay, a privileged journalist and friend of Kemal since the War of Independence, described in 1980 how, after Nuri's death, 'we could see that [Atatürk] had difficulty regarding his nervous balance. He had become very touchy.'[3] Atay adds that his close intimates had to behave very carefully at what he describes as 'the later part of his dining room activities'. Kemal was so restless that he hated to remain long in any particular residence; yet he continued to drink far too much raki and keep impossibly late hours, not only at Chankaya but in Istanbul and at Yalova, a spa resort on the Asian shore of the Sea of Marmara where he had a villa.

The yellowing skin of his face in these early months of 1937 made it look as if Atatürk was suffering from jaundice. He was, however, too quick-tempered to submit to strict medical control or allow his personal staff to seek expert advice from foreign specialists. His health had long been poor: chronic kidney trouble, recurrent bouts of malaria, and, as early as November 1923, the first of several mild heart attacks. There was, however, something different about his persistent debility in the summer of 1937: he had difficulty in standing for any length of time and complained of skin irritation, of head-aches, and of frequent nose bleeding which would not stop. As if to give the lie to tales of his failing health,

Atatürk deliberately asserted himself in public affairs, intervening personally in negotiations with France to secure autonomy for the Hatay, the region of Syria around Alexandretta and Antakya (biblical Antioch). He also encouraged the conclusion in July 1937 of a central Asian entente, the Saadabad Pact of friendship and non-aggression, which linked Turkey with Iraq, Iran and Afghanistan. Yet, rather curiously, Atatürk began to complain that he was being left out of government, that Prime Minister Ismet Inönü was treating him as an honor-ific president rather than as the maker and shaper of policy, at home and abroad.

By the time the Saadabad Pact was signed, Ismet had been prime minister for almost all of the past fifteen years. In character he was very different from Kemal, cautious, conscientious and staid, sober and abstemious, a dutiful family man whose growing deafness saved him from hearing the more barbed comments of his presi-dent. They had frequently differed over details of policy, but Kemal always trusted Ismet to carry out what was agreed between them, without making any startling innovations in home or foreign policy. Yet by the autumn of 1937 Ismet, too, was feeling the strain of office – the need for tact in transforming ideas, often broached as the raki was passed around in the small hours of the morn-ing, into practical proposals for executive action. One night at Chankaya in the third week of September 1937 Ismet lost his patience: 'How much longer is this country to be governed from a drunkard's table?' Ismet demanded.[4] Atatürk, surprised at the uncharacteristic outburst, let the moment pass peacefully; but next day, while he was travelling back to Istanbul in the presi-dential train, he sent for the prime minister and suggested it was time for him to take a rest. Turkish newspapers were informed that Ismet Inönü was leaving Ankara for a spell of sick leave. In the last week of October he handed over the premiership to Celâl Bayar.

Rumours of Atatürk's failing health were constantly denied. Not until January 1938 did he reluctantly accept the diagnosis of two physicians at Bursa, who told him that he was suffering from cirrhosis of the liver. Even so, on that evening he attended a ball at Bursa, ordered the orchestra to play some local folk music and personally joined in the dancing, which required occasionally going down on one knee to the floor, an exhausting activity for a man of fifty-seven, whatever the state of his health. Atatürk could not keep up the bravado. On 11 March 1938 the Turkish people were officially told that their president was seriously ill. A French specialist came to Chankaya and told Atatürk, in Bayar's presence, that with restraint and abstinence there was no reason why he should not live for another seven years.

He rested only briefly. At all costs he wanted to inspire the people of the Hatay with that sense of Turkish patriotism which was by now recognized as the essence of Kemalism. The Syrian Sanjak of Alexandretta was formally ceded to Turkey at midsummer in 1938 and handed over in the last week of July. Despite the intense heat Atatürk travelled south to Mersin and held military parades there, in Tarsus and later in Adana. The effort was too much for his constitution. When he returned to Ankara, he stayed in the capital for only two days, for even out at Chankaya he found it hard to breathe. In Istanbul he settled at first on his new presidential yacht. Soon, however, he had to accept that life was fast fading away. He was too ill for the train journey back to Ankara. Reluctantly he moved into the Sultan's old waterside palace.

The last weeks of Atatürk's life were therefore spent in a huge room on the second floor of the Dolmabahçe, his walnut bed placed parallel to the windows so that he could look out across the Bosphorus to the Anatolian shore. In recent months he had become reconciled to Ali Fuad (who had taken the surname Cebesoy); and the two men continued to discuss political affairs, and in particular the probability of a European war over Hitler's demands on Czechoslovakia. On the day that Hitler and Mussolini met the British and French prime ministers in Munich to conclude the agreement which sealed the fate of the Czechs, Atatürk was in a coma, his death expected at any hour. Yet, unexpectedly, he recovered consciousness. By Republic Day, a month later, he was still able to hear faintly the fireworks of national celebration and insisted on being taken in a chair to the windows.[5] He died twelve days later – at five minutes past nine on the morning of 10 November 1938. The clocks of the palace were stopped at that hour in tribute to his passing.

The long illness had enabled Atatürk to leave a clear testament for the future. He wished the Bayar government to remain in office but designated Ismet Inönü as his successor, even though Ismet had not seen him since April and remained in Ankara. Very properly, it was in the Turkish capital that Inönü formally assumed office as second president of the republic on 11 November.

Atatürk's embalmed body lay in state in the former throne room of the Dolmabahçe Palace. Nine days later, at Makbule Atadan's request, traditional Muslim funeral prayers were said for the one-time Ghazi before his coffin was carried on a gun-carriage to Sarayburnü Point and placed aboard the *Yavuz*. The veteran battle-cruiser then sailed out into the Sea of Marmara through lines of warships from foreign nations (including HMS *Malaya*, which had hurried the last Sultan into exile on another November morning sixteen years before). The coffin was brought ashore at Izmit and carried slowly by train along the railway which Atatürk and Inönü had defended in the critical months of the War of Independence; it passed through Eskişehir and on across the Sakarya River and beside the long hump of the Chal Dag to Ankara itself. There the coffin once again lay in state, outside the chamber of the Grand National Assembly, until at last, on

21 November, a second funeral procession brought
Atatürk's remains to a temporary marble tomb beneath
the dome of the Ethnography Museum. The long ritual
ceremonies of Muslim burial were waived. It was
announced that a fitting mausoleum would eventually be
built to honour the Father of the Republic; the site would
be determined by a special commission appointed by
President Inönü.

More pressing problems absorbed the immediate
attention of the politicians. How far should the form of
government change now that Atatürk was no longer able
to impose his will on the conduct of affairs? As a means
of safeguarding the essentials of Kemalism, in February
1937 the Grand National Assembly had incorporated the
basic tenets of the Republican People's Party as Article 2
in an amended Constitution. Inönü and Bayar were therefore committed to upholding six principles: republicanism; nationalism; democratic populism; revolutionary
dynamism; laicism; and étatism. Yet within this
programme there was considerable room for manoeuvre
and cautious experiment. At least two of the principles
were so vague that they defied close definition: 'revolutionary dynamism' implied the need to modify social
conditions so as to accommodate changing circumstances, rather than be hidebound to old conventions;
while 'étatism' was a form of partial state socialism,
which guaranteed the public ownership of heavy industry, public utilities and the means of communication.

Although the politicians were agreed that Turkey
should remain a secular state, Inönü was never so intran-
sigently anti-clerical, or laicist, as Atatürk and some
restraints on religious teaching were soon relaxed. Both
Inönü and Bayar recognized that the concept of 'democratic populism' also required qualification. Kemal had
spoken, as early as July 1920, of the need for 'government to pass into the hands of the people'. It was now
essential to broaden the institutions created during the

revolutionary years; there had already been tentative proposals for a second chamber in the Assembly as well as for a second political party, for secret ballot (not conceded until 1948) and for a guarantee that national minorities should be represented in the Assembly, either by direct vote or by the nomination of deputies. A modest change was made in the spring of 1939 and, by the end of that year, there were four spokesmen for minorities among the 429 members of the Grand National Assembly, while twenty-four deputies ranked as 'independents' within the Republican People's Party, an embryonic parliamentary opposition. Over the following eleven years Inönü presided over the transition from totalitarianism to an effective two-party system, finally stepping down after the elections of May 1950, in which a Democratic Party (led from 1946 onwards by the former prime minister, Celâl Bayar) won more than 53 per cent of the votes.

Yet throughout his presidential term Inönü's home policies were overshadowed by world crisis. Remarkably, Inönü and his gifted foreign minister, Sukru Saraçoglu, kept Turkey non-belligerent during World War II. Basically the Turks remained hostile to Germany and sympathetic to Great Britain, the United States and even to the old enemy, Greece. Inönü received Churchill on a visit to Adana in February 1943 and travelled to Cairo at the end of the year for a further meeting, where he emphasized his fears of future Soviet demands for a military presence on the Dardanelles. Eventually, in February 1945, Turkey declared war on Germany in order to qualify as a founder-member of the United Nations Organization, but the Turkish armed forces never went into action until the Korean War when, in November 1950, the Turkish brigade at Wawon was the first UN contingent to be attacked by the main Chinese Red Army.

Meanwhile, the Turkish government fostered an idealized concept of the 'Eternal Leader'. As early as 7 June

1939 the Mausoleum Commission announced that Ankara's Rasattepe ('Observation Hill') would become Atatürk's final resting place. In November 1943 – while the attention of the world was concentrated on great battles in the Ukraine and southern Italy – the Turkish Press reported that the plan of two architects, Emin Onat and Orhan Arda, had been chosen from forty-nine designs submitted to the commission. Even so, another ten years passed before, on 10 November 1953, Atatürk's coffin was brought by gun-carriage from the Ethnography Museum to the landscaped hill, once a wild spot where Kemal had sometimes amused himself in the early morning by hunting rabbits with his friend Nuri Conker.

Henceforth Rasattepe was known as Anittepe ('Mausoleum Hill'). It became a revolutionary shrine, like Lenin's cavern-like vault in Moscow's Red Square, although more spacious and dignified. Atatürk had particularly encouraged afforestation on the slopes of the denuded Anatolian hills and the Anittepe was planted with trees sent from numerous foreign lands. Twenty-four Hittite lions – a form of statuary from the oldest civilization known to have flourished in central Anatolia – flanked the avenue up to a huge ceremonial parade ground on the levelled summit of the hill. Around the parade ground was a colonnade linking eight low towers which recalled aspects of Kemal's achievements. Twelve inscribed sayings look down from the walls. Among them are 'The waging of war when the life of the nation is not under threat is a murderous crime' and 'A nation that has no national pride is prey for other nations'. The mausoleum (Anitkabir), a neo-classical temple, was higher than any building in Ankara when it was completed; it dominated the skyline, complementing the Hisar, the twelfth-century hilltop citadel a mile and a half away, across the sprawling old town. For Turks and visiting foreign dignitaries the Anitkabir became a place of dutiful pilgrimage.

Kemal's uncompromising drive to Westernize his

country had aroused interest among Turkey's neighbours long before his health finally gave way. The first foreign country to import a modified Kemalism was Iran. Until 1905 Persia (as Iran was officially called before 1935) had experienced a similar system of government to the un-reformed Ottoman Empire, although the shahs of the ruling Qajar dynasty never possessed the religious authority claimed by the sultans as caliphs. After nearly twenty years of faltering experiments in parliamentary government the Qajar dynasty was overthrown in a military coup led by Colonel Reza Khan in October 1925. The Colonel, a choleric commander of the Persian Cossack Brigade, frequently expressed admiration for Kemal, both as a person and as a ruler, although he had none of the Ghazi's experience of military campaigns. Like Kemal, he proposed to modernize his country but, instead of accepting republicanism, the colonel was himself proclaimed Shah of Iran six weeks after his coup and made the throne hereditary in his family, substituting the Pahlevi dynasty for the discredited Qajars.

Reza Shah duly visited Turkey in 1934 and was entertained by Kemal, who impressed him with the progress of Westernization in the republic. On returning to Teheran, the Shah sought to copy much of what he had seen in Turkey: he imposed European costume, French and Swiss codes of law, built schools, developed roads and railways, and – a sure, but superficial, sign of Kemal's influence – at once ordered the building of an opera house in his capital. But Reza Shah's years as ruler of Iran are of greatest interest in showing how easily Kemal could have misused his privileged post. For the Shah accumulated great personal wealth through appropriating the best land in his kingdom. Three years after Atatürk's death, allied suspicion that the Shah was in the pay of Nazi Germany led to a joint Anglo-Soviet occupation of Iran in September 1941 and the proclamation of Reza Shah's son, Muhammad Reza Pahlevi, as ruler of the country. He remained on the 'Peacock Throne' until deposed in March 1979, after the Ayatollah Khomeini established his Islamic Republic in Teheran.

Muhammad Reza Pahlevi attempted to Westernize Iran more thoroughly than his father, especially after 1953 when he concentrated power in his own hands. Much that was achieved remained cosmetic and owed more to a glossy image of America than to the western European culture which Atatürk had admired, if not always understood. Yet, like Kemal, the Shah at first graciously imposed liberal reforms: he permitted experiments in party government in 1962 and again between 1964 and March 1975; and he then belatedly tried to organize a single 'National Resurrection Party' on Kemalist principles, although without any concessions to republicanism. Iranian women were formally and legally emancipated in 1963; and in January of that year the Shah's social reform programme received 5.6 million votes in a national referendum against a mere 4115 vote opposition.

Ultimately, however, the Shah failed disastrously. Although he imposed the land reforms which his father had neglected, oil revenue allowed him to continue to display great wealth among a people still suffering from rural poverty and widespread illiteracy. The Shah lacked Atatürk's canny perception of what was socially acceptable and he made no protracted attempt to prepare his countrymen for change by education and example. His ministry of public instruction administered the charitable and educational institutions attached to the mosques, but neither of the Pahlevi Shahs dared secularize Iran. In seeking to diminish the authority of the Shia fundamentalists, the central government in Teheran stimulated a fanatical response which – unlike the dervishes – was able to harness a republican xenophobia such as could never have existed in Kemal's Turkey. Muslim puritan hostility to 'Western degeneracy' united with student protests at the Shah's lack of sympathy with

the Arab cause and his role as 'a tool of Western capital-
ism'. This formidable force, unexpectedly finding a charismatic leader in an octogenarian Ayatollah, then turned
against Iran's ruling Establishment.

The fallen Shah died from cancer in July 1980 as an
exile in Cairo, where he was given sanctuary by President
Anwar al-Sadat, one of Atatürk's warmest admirers. Sadat
– who, like Gamel Abdel Nasser, was born in the year
World War I ended – recalled in his memoirs how in the
1920s Mustafa Kemal's portrait hung on the wall of his
parents' home in Lower Egypt and how his father had
taught him that the President of Turkey was a great man,
a brave soldier who had freed his country from foreign
domination.[6] Nasser, too, held Atatürk in respect. It is not
surprising that the Egyptian Revolution of 1952–54 had
closer parallels with the Turkish experience than with
any other national upheaval, the Nasser–Sadat partnership coming to resemble the relationship between Kemal
and Ismet Inönü; for in King Farouk's Egypt, as in the
Ottoman Empire, a radical nationalism spread rapidly
among young army officers who were fired by contempt
for a feeble monarchy, resented foreign control over the
economy, and were indignant at a military defeat inflicted
by a despised enemy.

President Nasser and his successors in Egypt followed
Kemalist principles in sweeping away many practices
which perpetuated the old social order. Nasser encouraged indirect popular participation in government and he
evolved a form of 'étatism' which favoured the supervision of state public work schemes, cooperatives and
enterprises which were under private ownership within a
planned national economy. There were, however, significant differences between the Turkish and Egyptian
movements. Since Nasser sought to create a 'United Arab
Republic', the Egyptian people were bound by their
constitution to accept a Pan-Arab nationalism, with Islam
as a state religion, and Arabic as the official language.

Moreover, at least so long as Nasser lived, it was expedient to emphasize the 'democratic socialist' character of his republic in order to retain the backing of the Soviet Union and a primacy among other revolutionary movements, notably in Syria and along the southern shores of the Mediterranean.

Later instances of militant Arab republicanism – Gaddafi's curious experiment with a dictatorial 'direct democracy' in Libya and the pragmatic Ba'ath Socialism of Iraq's Saddam Hussein, in particular – owe even less to the Turkish experience. Like Kemal, both Gaddafi and Saddam recognized the regenerative effect of nationalist sentiment on a demoralized people. But neither possesses that heroic quality of leadership which enabled Kemal to channel patriotic pride into constructive reform rather than external aggression. For, however much Atatürk may have set a precedent for the Shah of Iran and other neighbouring leaders, Kemalism was never intended for export. The basic six principles were determined by Turkey's needs in the 1920s and 1930s, when there were no extra-European superpowers, no threat of nuclear disaster, no Common Market or Comecon, no independent republic of Israel, and no militant Islamic movement capable of challenging the prevailing mood of secularism. Since 1950, when the Democratic Party's electoral victory brought Celâl Bayar to the presidency in succession to Inönü, Turkish leaders have sought constantly to accommodate their policies within what they claim to be the natural evolutionary pattern of Kemalism.

Not surprisingly, there have been wide variations in these interpretations of Kemalism. Atatürk himself always believed that, except at moments of grave danger to the nation, the army should stay outside politics. His insistence on wearing formal civilian dress on state occasions – top hat, black tail-coat, white tie – rather than the uniform of a field marshal was a gesture of reassurance, a denial that he wished to govern through military dictatorship. It was therefore natural that the Democratic Party under President Celâl Bayar and his prime minister, Adnan Menderes, should seek to preserve the civilian character of government for the remainder of the multi-party experiment, which continued until April 1960. Menderes, a lawyer born in Smyrna in 1899, had received much of his schooling from American teachers. His government strengthened Turkey's links with western Europe, joining NATO in 1952. A year later Bayar and Menderes presided over the reinterment of Atatürk's remains in Ankara's marble mausoleum, thereby associat-ing the 'Eternal Leader' with the Democratic Party regime. However, as Menderes relied to a greater extent than his predecessors on peasant support, traditional Kemalists – and university students – accused him of allowing Muslim religious organizations to recover some of their lost influence in rural areas. At the same time, he was criticized for his failure to keep inflation in check, while his willingness to negotiate with Great Britain and Greece over Cyprus gradually lost him the support of senior army officers. The unfortunate Menderes survived an air crash at Gatwick in February 1959, only to be over-thrown fifteen months later by the National Unity Committee, a group of army officers led by General Cemal Gursel, who then charged Menderes with unconsti-tutional practices. He was put on trial and hanged. From October 1961 until March 1966 Genral Gursel served as Turkey's fourth president, with Ismet Inönü again in office as prime minister until February 1965.

The National Unity Committee dissolved the Grand National Assembly in the last week of May 1960 and sought the preparation of a new constitution by a team of jurists. Theoretically the subsequent 1961 constitution consolidated Kemal's revolution, emphasizing the secular and Westernized character of the state and the emanci-pation of women. It separated the legislature and execu-tive, instituted a constitutional court, and offered guarantees of basic rights and freedoms under an independent judiciary. One of its principal architects, Professor Muammer Aksoy, looking back on his blueprint for defending social democracy more than a quarter of a century later, claimed that the 1961 constitution corresponded closely to the needs of Turkish society at that time, because 'it was secular and loyal to Atatürk's reforms'; and in a national referendum (9 July 1961) the Turkish people gave their new constitution warm approval.[7]

Ten years later, however, the basic assumptions behind the 1961 constitution were again being questioned, particularly by the army. The generals complained that, instead of the strong presidential leadership which the republic had received from Atatürk and İnönü, the constitution favoured weak coalitions. The army intervened again in politics in March 1971, securing substantial revision of the constitution, including amendments to no less than thirty-five of its articles. Even so, by the end of the decade, the authority of the state was questioned in many of the republic's provinces: there was fighting at the universities between right-wing and left-wing students; Shiites sought to assert an Islamic puritanism alien to most Turkish believers as well as to the secularist politicians; and there were frequent clashes between the Turkish authorities and Kurdish and Armenian separatists. In September 1980 the Turkish army intervened in politics for the third time in eleven years. A six-man National Security Council, headed by General Kenan Evren, seized power and remained the political dynamo of the republic until December 1983. A second commission of jurists, under the chairmanship of Professor Orhan Aldikacti, provided Turkey with the constitution of November 1982, which broadened the powers of the president, in the belief that the republic needed that decisive executive leadership still associated with the memory of Atatürk.

No sooner had General Evren come to power in September 1980 than he sought publicly to link his regime with the founder of the republic. General Evren insisted, in a national appeal relayed by state television and radio, that the army command had taken over the government so as to 'protect the youth of our country ... from deviating away from Atatürk's ideal'; and one of the first acts of the National Security Council was a collective pilgrimage to the marble tomb at the Anitkabir. There General Evren not only laid a wreath in Atatürk's honour, but in the distinguished visitors' book wrote an open letter to the deified leader: the letter explained that, as a trustee for his ideals, the Turkish army had intervened in politics in order to call a halt to those who were propelling the Turkish nation into an abyss of 'darkness and helplessness'.[8]

There were moments, during the following decade, when those who had believed that Atatürk and Inönü always sought to guide Turkey towards a liberal democracy began to question the right of the army leaders to exercise this trusteeship they had assumed. Repeated evidence of a Turkish denial of basic human rights and of harsh prison conditions led to protests from Amnesty International and, since writers and publishers suffered particularly severely, from PEN International, too. Although General Evren gradually relaxed martial law and, in the closing weeks of 1983, dissolved the six-man National Security Council with which he had seized power, it was another six years before the republic had a civilian president – for only the second time in its history. In November 1989 Turgut Ozal, a much criticized prime minister since 1983, moved into the presidential palace, while Yildirim Akbulut formed a predominantly 'Motherland Party' government. In 1989, too, Turkey at last recognized the jurisdiction of the European Court of Human Rights and ratified conventions banning the use of torture. Even so, the guerrilla war waged by the PKK

(Kurdish Workers Party) in the predominantly Kurdish-speaking, south-eastern part of the republic has kept eight of Turkey's seventy-one provinces under emergency rule since 1987, as well as costing the lives of more than two thousand people.[9]

The problem of the Kurds – or 'mountain Turks', as they are called officially – was familiar to Kemal. He would, however, have been surprised by the extent of the Kurdish rebellion in 1989–90 and perplexed by the difficulties facing the authorities as they sought to safeguard orderly lives for the people of Diyarbekir and other towns along the Syrian border. Almost certainly Atatürk would approve of the attempts by President Ozal and Prime Minister Akbulut to secure Turkey's entry into the EEC, for he was a firm believer in collective agreements and in regional pacts designed to promote peace and reconciliation between potential enemies. He would be puzzled at the presence in the government of a strict believer in Islamic traditions, at the size of the new Kocatepe Mosque barely a mile from his Anittepe Mausoleum, and at the return of Islamic piety to many university students. Few people, even a decade ago, would have predicted the emergence of a Muslim pressure group prepared to urge the Grand National Assembly to repeal an order which had banned the wearing by young women of enveloping headscarves at university lectures and official functions. Fifty years after Atatürk's death the laicism of his secular state was on the defensive.

Yet at each crisis in the republic's affairs, a legendary Kemal Atatürk is invoked as the saviour of the Turkish people. In other lands past leaders frequently fall from grace soon after their death: statues are toppled, pictures consigned to the flames, their cult of personality is condemned, their achievements are minimized or discredited. But not Atatürk: his memory continues to be revered as the spark which brought life to the nation. 'How happy is the man who can say he is a Turk,' one of the simplest of Kemal's sayings, remains a commonplace slogan, even if, to outsiders, the combination of high inflation and a population explosion often seems to give an ironic twist to his proud claim. When a new dam irrigates the parched soil between the upper Tigris and Euphrates this vast public works project will carry Atatürk's name. So already do bridges, motorways and city boulevards constructed long after his death. His sculptured bust stands outside railway stations and beside landing quays; his statue, often depicting him as a teacher of the young, looks out over public squares and parks. And still, at five minutes after nine in the morning of 10 November each year, the entire nation observes a minute's silence in memory of the leader whom less than one in five of the population can remember as a living person. Then, when the minute expires, horns and whistles and sirens break the rare moment of peace so as to emphasize to the world that, whatever imperfections remain in its system of government, the republic which Mustafa Kemal created out of a fallen empire and a backward people is set to survive the century in which he brought it into being.

References

Abbreviations

Kinross: Lord Kinross, *Atatürk, The Rebirth of a Nation* (London: Weidenfeld & Nicolson 1964).

Shaw & Shaw: S.J. Shaw and E.K. Shaw, *History of the Ottoman Empire and the Turkish Republic*, Vol. 2 (Cambridge: Cambridge University Press 1977).

Speech: M.K. Atatürk, *A Speech delivered by Ghazi Mustapha Kemal, President of the Turkish Republic, October 1927* (Leipzig: 1929).

Volkan & Itzkowitz: V.D. Volkan and N. Itzkowitz, *The Immortal Atatürk* (Chicago and London: University of Chicago Press 1984).

Introduction

1. For Nesselrode and the changes in Russian policy see A. Palmer, *The Chancelleries of Europe* (London: Allen and Unwin 1983) pp. 51–2 and M.S. Anderson, *The Eastern Question, 1774–1923* (London: Macmillan 1966) p. 71.

2. The diary kept by the ambassador (Seymour), now in the British Library (Add. MSS 60306), adds new material to this well-known episode. See A. Palmer, *The Banner of Battle* (London: Weidenfeld & Nicolson 1987) pp. 13–15.

3. Stratford de Redcliffe, *The Eastern Question* (London,

1881), p. 49. This book, published soon after Stratford's death in 1880, reprints articles and letters which he wrote during the Eastern Crisis of 1875–8.

Chapter 1

1. A.P. Vacalopoulos, *A History of Thessaloniki* (Salonika, 1963), p. 114.
2. Kemal's childhood reminiscences were given to the Turkish journalist Ahmed Emin in an interview published in the newspaper *Vakit*, 10 January 1922. There have been several English extracts; see Volkan & Itzkowitz p. 29.
3. cf. H.C. Armstrong, *Grey Wolf* (Harmondsworth: Penguin 1939) p. 29.
4. A. Palmer, *The Kaiser* (London: Weidenfeld and Nicolson 1976) pp. 91–2.
5. I. and M. Orga, *Atatürk* (London: Michael Joseph 1962) pp. 22–3.
6. Shaw & Shaw pp. 264–5.
7. There is dispute over Kemal's commitment to the Young Turks; cf. E.E. Ramsaur, *The Young Turks* (Princeton: Princeton University Press 1957) pp. 95–6 with F. Ahmad, *The Young Turks* (Oxford: Oxford University Press 1969) pp. 45–6.
8. Volkan & Itzkowitz pp. 62–3; Ahmad, op. cit. pp. 1–13.
9. Shaw & Shaw pp. 280–82.
10. For Kemal in France, Kinross p. 42; for Enver's English contacts, M. Gilbert, *Winston S. Churchill* Vol. 3 p. 189 and Companion Vol. 3 Pt. 1, p. 39 (London: Heinemann 1971, 1972).
11. One of the few accounts of the campaign is G.F. Abbott, *The Holy War in Tripoli* (London: E. Arnold 1912).
12. Kinross pp. 54–5.
13. Shaw & Shaw p. 295.
14. F. Fischer, *War of Illusions* (London: Chatto and

Windus 1975) pp. 332–4, using material from the German archives.

15. Volkan & Itzkowitz pp. 76–8, using both Turkish and Bulgarian material.

Chapter 2

1. Liman von Sanders, *Five Years in Turkey* (Annapolis, Maryland: US Naval Institute 1927) may be supplemented by the memoirs of one of his staff, Colonel Hans Kannengeisser, *The Campaign in Gallipoli* (London: Hutchinson 1927).

2. Kemal's reminiscences, given originally in an interview to R.E. Unaydin and published in Istanbul in 1930, have frequently appeared in English translations, notably in R. Rhodes James, *Gallipoli* (London: Papermac ed. 1989) pp. 112–13 and in B. Pitt (ed.), *History of the First World War*, II, no. 12 (London: BPC 1966) pp. 774–7. See also Volkan & Itzkowitz p. 87 and Kinross p. 75; compare the assessment in C.F. Aspinall-Oglander, *Military Operations: Gallipoli* (London: Heinemann 1929–32), pp. 120–1.

3. Kinross p. 78.

4. For the shattered watch and Turkish accounts of the episode see Volkan & Itzkowitz pp. 89–90. The diary extract is from Compton Mackenzie, *Gallipoli Memories* (London: Panther 1965) p. 301. See also the respect for the Turkish defence shown by John Churchill in a letter home to his brother, Winston, 11 August 1915, M. Gilbert, *Winston S. Churchill*, Companion Vol. 3 Pt. 2 (London: Heinemann 1971), pp. 1125–30.

5. Aspinall-Oglander, *op. cit.* pp. 485–6.

6. Volkan & Itzkowitz pp. 93–4.

7. Franz von Papen, *Memoirs* (London: Deutsch 1952) p. 74.

8. Kinross pp. 105–6.

9. Volkan & Itzkowitz p. 101.
10. J.W. Wheeler-Bennett, *Hindenburg, The Wooden Titan* (London: Macmillan 1936) p. 145.
11. Volkan & Itzkowitz pp. 103–5. Turkish historians emphasize the importance of the visit to Carlsbad, pointing out that the sojourn gave Kemal the first opportunity to marshal his thoughts since he became a national hero; Ayse Afetinan, *M. Kemal Atatürk ün Karlsbad hatiralari* (Ankara 1983).
12. Kinross pp. 117–19. For a short British account of the campaign, C. Falls, *Armageddon* (London: Batsford 1964).
13. Volkan & Itzkowitz p. 108.
14. Kinross p. 153.

Chapter 3

1. H. Nicolson, *Peacemaking 1919* (London: Constable 1933) emphasizes the influence of Venizelos. See also D. Walder, *The Chanak Affair* (London: Hutchinson 1969) p. 66.
2. Volkan & Itzkowitz pp. 110–17 has a full account of Kemal's activities in this period; but, to sense the mood and privations of the time, see Halide Edib, *The Turkish Ordeal* (London: John Murray 1928) pp. 7–18 and Irfan Orga, *Portrait of a Turkish Family* (London: Eland 1988) pp. 188, 194, 201.
3. Volkan & Itzkowitz p. 124, citing the definitive edition of Atatürk's wartime reminiscences, F.R. Atay, *Atatürk'ün Hatiralari 1914–1919* (Ankara 1965).
4. Kemal described his actions at this time in great detail in 1927, Speech pp. 24–57.
5. Speech pp. 76–121; B. Lewis, *The Emergence of Modern Turkey (London: RIIA 1971) pp. 242–5.*
6. *Edib, op. cit.*, pp. 53–62; Kinross p. 202 and pp. 208–9.
7. Edib, *op. cit.*, pp. 65–124 her escape across Anatolia; pp. 135–50 the mood in Ankara. The National Assembly

building is now the War of Independence Museum; a brochure in English, published by the Ankara Chamber of Commerce, is informative.

8. E.G. Mears and others, *Modern Turkey* (New York, 1924) pp. 634–42; M. Gilbert, *Winston S. Churchill* (London: Heinemann 1985) Vol. 4, pp. 479, 482, 486–7.

9. There is no detailed study in English of the Turko-Greek War, but Kinross pp. 231–319 includes seven chapters dealing with the main battles. See Shaw & Shaw pp. 358ff and 460–1 for Turkish sources, supplemented by several hundred pages of the Speech. Prince Andrew of Greece, *Towards Disaster* (London: John Murray 1930) gives a deeply moving Greek account of the campaign.

10. Volkan & Itzkowitz p. 194; Speech pp. 564–6.

11. This report was reprinted in G. Ward Price, *Extra-Special Correspondent* (London: Harrap 1957) p. 129.

12. Sir Charles Harington, *Tim Harington Looks Back* (London: John Murray 1940) pp. 100–59.

13. Martin Gilbert, *Winston S. Churchill*, Vol. 4, p. 821.

14. *Ibid.*, p. 854, forming part of a comprehensive and concise Chapter 45 on Chanak. See also David Walder, *The Chanak Affair* (London: Hutchinson 1969) pp. 303–18.

Chapter 4

1. Kinross pp. 344–6.

2. C. Harington, *Tim Harington Looks Back*, pp. 129–31.

3. See H. Nicolson, *Curzon, The Last Phase* (London: Constable 1934) pp. 281–350; R. Davison, 'Turkish Diplomacy from Mudros to Lausanne', forming Chapter 6 of G.A. Craig & F. Gilbert, *The Diplomats* (Princeton: Princeton University Press 1953).

4. Kinross pp. 362–3; Volkan & Itzkowitz pp. 229, 263.

5. See the brochure cited in Note 7, Chapter 3. Extracts

from Atatürk's speeches are printed, in French, in G.D. Turbecki, *Universalité de la Pensée d'Atatürk* (Ankara: AFIST, 1982) pp. 11–27.

6. Shaw & Shaw pp. 369, 374–5, 380, 384; Kinross p. 384–6.
7. Shaw & Shaw pp. 380–81; Volkan & Itzkowitz pp. 247–8; Kinross pp. 394–5.
8. Kinross p. 402.
9. Extracts from these speeches are in Volkan & Itzkowitz p. 255 and B. Lewis, *The Emergence of Modern Turkey*, p. 263.
10. Atatürk, *Söylev ve Demecleri* (Ankara: TITE, 1959) Vol. II, p. 243.
11. Kinross Chapter 52; Volkan & Itzkowitz pp. 262–8; cf., more critically, I. & M. Orga, *Atatürk* (London: Michael Joseph 1962) pp. 266–71.
12. Atatürk, *op. cit.*, p. 249.
13. Kinross p. 439.
14. Speech pp. 723–4.

Chapter 5

1. The fullest treatment of these aspects of Atatürk's private life in English, but using Turkish sources, is in the 'psychobiography' of Volkan & Itzkowitz, especially pp. 166–8, 182–3, 205–6, 208–10 and 235 for Fikriye and pp. 202–4, 219 and 250 for Latife. But see also Orga, *op. cit.*, pp. 208–12 and 244–8.
2. Volkan & Itzkowitz pp. 293–4. On the Turkish State Ballet see Ninette de Valois, *Step by Step* (London: Allen 1977) pp. 165–70.
3. Kinross pp. 471–2, 485, 494, 497; Volkan & Itzkowitz pp. 276–7, 315.
4. See the extract, and description, in Volkan & Itzkowitz p. 284.
5. *Ibid.*, p. 285, citing H. Yücebaş, *Atatürk'ün nükteleri-fikralari-hatiralari* (Istanbul: KK 1963) pp. 15–20.

6. Kinross pp. 450–7.
7. Volkan & Itzkowitz p. 291.
8. C.A. Macartney & A.W. Palmer, *Independent Eastern Europe* (London: Macmillan 1962) pp. 1175–6.
9. A. Eden, *Facing the Dictators* (London: Cassell 1962) p. 469.
10. Extracts from a perceptive lecture by Sir Percy Loraine, given at Edinburgh in 1948, are printed in B. Tuncel (ed.), *Atatürk 1881–1938* (Ankara: UNESCO 1963) pp. 216–23.
11. Duke of Windsor, *A King's Story* (London: Cassell 1960), pp. 309–11.
12. For the Grey Wolf legend see Volkan & Itzkowitz p. 200.

Chapter 6

1. Windsor, *King's Story*, p. 310.
2. Loraine lecture, in Tuncel (ed.), *Atatürk*, p. 217.
3. Volkan & Itzkowitz p. 332 citing Falih Rifki Atay's book *Çankaya* (Istanbul, 1980 edition). Extracts from the 1961 edition of Atay's reminiscences are in the Tuncel book, cited above, pp. 127–30.
4. This version is taken from Kinross p. 486, who interviewed Ismet. Other accounts of the incident, deriving from Selek and Atay, show only slight variations: Volkan & Itzkowitz p. 335.
5. Kinross pp. 497–8. For the impression made by Atatürk's illness and death on the Turkish people, see Irfan Orga, *Portrait of a Turkish Family*, pp. 275–7.
6. A. el-Sadat, *In Search of Identity*, (London: Hutchinson 1978) pp. 12, 16.
7. Muammer Aksoy, quoted in *Turkish Daily News*, 25 September 1989, p. B 8. This issue also contained an interview with Professor Aldikacti on the structure of the 1982 Constitution.
8. On Evren, Volkan & Itzkowitz pp. 353–4.

References

9. For a shrewd analysis of the revived Kurdish threat to the Turkish Republic, see the article by Hugh Pope in *The Independent* (London) 7 April 1990, p. 13, sent from Nusaybin.

Select Bibliography

The best English language biography of Mustafa Kemal is Lord Kinross, *Atatürk: The Rebirth of a Nation* (London: Weidenfeld & Nicolson 1964; New York: W. Morrow 1965). Also useful are Irfan Orga, *Phoenix Ascendant: The Rise of Modern Turkey* (London: Robert Hale 1958), Irfan and Margarete Orga, *Atatürk* (London: Michael Joseph 1962) and, more sensationally, R. Brock, *Ghost on Horseback, The Incredible Atatürk* (New York: Duel, Sloan and Pearce 1954). The famous pioneer biography H.C. Armstrong, *Grey Wolf* (various editions since 1932), although long since outdated, has some value for its use of Turkish material printed during Atatürk's lifetime. V.D. Volkan and N. Itzkowitz, *The Immortal Atatürk* (Chicago and London: University of Chicago Press 1984) is subtitled 'a psychobiography'; even to a sceptical non-Freudian it remains a stimulating study, especially interesting because of its use of little-known material from the memoirs of people who were in close touch with Kemal. An earlier book using some Turkish sources is Elaine D. Smith, *Turkey, Origins of the Kemalist Movement and the Government of the Grand National Assembly, 1919–1923* (Washington, 1959).

For both the general background and a good summary of Kemal's achievements, see Bernard Lewis, *The Emergence of Modern Turkey* (Oxford: Oxford University Press 1968; London: RIIA 1971 paperback). The seminal study on Turkish history from 1808 to 1975 remains Stanford J. Shaw and Ezel Kural Shaw, *History of the Ottoman Empire and Modern Turkey*, Volume 2, which is subtitled *Reform, Revolution and Republic* (Cambridge: Cambridge University Press 1977). For the Asian Question see M.E. Yapp, *The Making of the Modern Near East 1792–1923* (London: Longman 1987). The controversial Elie Kedourie's *England and the Middle East: The Destruction of the Ottoman Empire 1914–21* (London: Mansell 1987 and Westview Press, Colorado) was first published in 1956 but the book has been reissued with a new hard-hitting introduction. It may now be supplemented by David Fromkin, *A Peace to End All Peace: Creating the Modern Middle East, 1914–22* (London: Deutsch 1989). M.S. Anderson, *The Eastern Question, 1774–1923* (London: Macmillan 1966; New York: St Martin's Press 1966) and C.A. Macartney & A.W. Palmer, *Independent Eastern Europe* (London: Macmillan 1962) also cover a geographically wide area. A. Emin, *Turkey in the World War* (New Haven: Yale University Press 1930) is concerned with the social effect of the war rather than with the campaigns. R. Rhodes James, *Gallipoli* (London: Batsford 1965) has been reissued in a Papermac edition (Basingstoke: Macmillan 1989). See also Martin Gilbert, *Churchill*, Vol. 3 (London: Heinemann 1971). On the Chanak Crisis see David Walder, *The Chanak Affair* (London: Hutchinson 1969).

Three extremely readable books of wide interest are Halide Edib, *Memoirs* (London: J. Murray 1926; New York: Century 1926) and her *The Turkish Ordeal* (London: J. Murray 1928), and Irfan Orga, *Portrait of a Turkish Family*, first published in London by Gollancz in 1950 but reissued with an interesting family 'Afterword' (London: Eland; New York: Hippocrene 1988).

Kemal Atatürk's long-running speech of October 1927 was published in an English translation in Leipzig, 1929. Abraham Bodurgil, *Kemal Atatürk: A Centennial Bibliography* (Washington DC: Library of Congress 1984) contains details of over 2,000 works in western languages on Kemal's life and times. For Turkish readers the great source is K.Z. Gencosman & N.A. Banõglu, *Atatürk ansiklopedisi* (Istanbul, 1981, ten volumes).

Index

Index

Index

Index

Index

Index